MIL-HDBK-511
15 May 2000

DEPARTMENT OF DEFENSE HANDBOOK
FOR
INTEROPERABILITY OF INTERACTIVE
ELECTRONIC TECHNICAL MANUALS (IETMs)

This handbook is for guidance only. Do not cite this document as a requirement.

FOREWORD

1. This handbook is approved for use by all Departments and Agencies of the Department of Defense.

2. Beneficial comments (recommendations, additions, deletions) and any pertinent data which may be of use in improving this document should be addressed to: Commander, USAMC Logistics Support Activity, ATTN: AMXLS-AP, Redstone Arsenal, AL 35898-7466 by using the Standardization Document Improvement Proposal (DD Form 1426) appearing at the end of this document or by letter.

3. This handbook cannot be cited as a requirement. If it is, the contractor does not have to comply.

CONTENTS

PARAGRAPH   PAGE

FOREWORD ii

1.0   SCOPE.. 1
1.1   Scope... 1
1.2   Application.. 1
1.3   Background 2
1.3.1   Tri-Service Approach to Solving the Problem................... 3
1.3.2   Objective and Primary Goal for the Architecture 3

2.0   APPLICABLE DOCUMENTS..................................... 4
2.1   General.. 4
2.2   Government documents.. 4
2.2.1   Specifications, Standards, and Handbooks 4
2.3   Non-Government Publications 5
2.4   Order of Precedence.. 5

3.0   DEFINITIONS... 5
3.1   Acronyms Used in this Handbook 5
3.2   Definitions of Selected Terms 7

4.0   GENERAL GUIDANCE 10
4.1   Overview of the Joint IETM Architecture 10
4.1.1   Overall Joint IETM Architecture Concept....................... 10
4.1.2   Basic Architecture Independent of Operating Systems...... 13
4.1.3   Developing a Solution for IETM Interoperability............. 13
4.2   Characteristics of the Architecture which should be preserved
                in Future JIA Implementations...................................... 13
4.2.1   Characteristics of the JIA for the User............................ 13
4.2.2   Characteristics of the JIA to be Maintained by the IETM
                Developer.. 16
4.2.3   Characteristics of the JIA for the DoD IETM Distribution
                Infrastructure 16
4.3   Summary of Recommendations for Implementation of the
                Joint IETM Architecture 18
4.3.1   Common Browser 18
4.3.2   Object Encapsulation and Component Interface............... 19
4.3.3   Electronic Addressing and Library Functions.................. 19
4.3.4   Intranet Server and Database Server Interface................. 20
4.4   Communications Security and Information Assurance
                Recommendations 20
4.5   Permitting IETM use in a Stand-Alone Environment........ 21

CONTENTS

PARAGRAPH   PAGE

4.5.1   Occasionally-Connected User Devices   21
4.5.2   Dual-Mode IETMs   21

5.0   BROWSER COMPONENTS   22
5.1   Overview   22
5.2   Classification   22
5.3   Salient Characteristics   23
5.3.1   Thin Client/Server Model   24
5.3.2   Commercially Defined Object Model   24
5.3.3   Commonly Used Internet Transport and Addressing Protocols   24
5.3.4   Frames   24
5.3.5   Extensible Components   24
5.3.6   User Interface   24
5.3.7   Offline Browsing   24
5.3.8   HTML Support   25
5.3.9   Security   25
5.3.10   Java   25
5.3.11   Supported Data Types   25
5.3.12   Multimedia   26
5.4   Implementing Advanced Features   26
5.4.1   eXtensible Markup Language (XML)   26
5.4.2   Java   26
5.5   Regulatory Guidance   26

6.0   OBJECT ENCAPULATION GUIDANCE   26
6.1   Core Object Encapsulation   27
6.2   Object Encapsulation for various JIA Architecture Types   27
6.2.1   Properties of Client-based Architecture Types   30
6.2.2   Properties of Server-based Architecture Types   31
6.2.3   General Advisory for the Development of the Differing
             Architecture Types   33

7.0   IETM ADDRESSING AND REGISTRY SOFTWARE   35
7.1   General   35
7.1.1   Background   35
7.1.2   Recommended Operational Capability   35
7.1.3   Operational Environments   35
7.1.4   Security Environment   36
7.1.5   Life Cycle Support   36
7.2   Salient Characteristics of External Entity Addresses   36
7.2.1   External Entity Address Description   36

CONTENTS

PARAGRAPH   PAGE

7.2.2   External Entity Address Features/Benefits 37
7.2.3   External Entity Address Specifications.. 37
7.2.4   Minimum Criteria for External Addressing of Entities and
           Catalog Registry.. 38
7.2.5   Virtual Uniform Resource Locator 38
7.2.6   Other vURL attributes.. 39
7.3   Initial Guidance for Establishing and Using vURLs......................... 39
7.4   IETM Object Metadata.. 41
7.5   Metadata... 41
7.6   Search Engine 41
7.7   IETM Component Registry Description... 41
7.7.1   Background 41
7.7.2   Recommended Operational Capability 42
7.7.3   Life Cycle Support... 42
7.8   IETM Object Registry Features/Benefits... 42
7.9   IETM Object Registry Specifications 43
7.10   URLs and File Pathname Locators for Legacy Applications............. 43
7.11   Service Points of Contact for vURL Registration............................. 44

8.0   WEB SERVER/CLIENT/STAND-ALONE IMPLEMENTATION
           GUIDANCE.. 44
8.1   Overview 44
8.1.1   The Joint IETM Architecture 44
8.1.2   Connectivity of IETMs... 45
8.1.3   Off-the-Shelf Web Servers 45
8.1.4   Legacy IETM Systems 45
8.2   Networked Client/Server IETM Applications..................................... 45
8.2.1   Web Server Support and Implementation... 46
8.2.1.1   The Networked Approach.. 46
8.2.1.2   Use of Customized Server Applications and/or Extensions.............. 46
8.2.1.3   Networked Client/Server Configuration Features............................. 47
8.2.2   Database-driven IETM Applications 47
8.2.3   Application Development Considerations 48
8.2.3.1   Servers and Server-side Applications 48
8.2.3.2   Installation of Multiple Web Servers or Multiple Database
           Servers... 48
8.3   Occasionally Connected IETM Applications...................................... 48
8.3.1   Web Server Support and Implementation... 49
8.3.2   Addressing in the Occasionally Connected Mode 49
8.3.3   Occasionally Connected Mode Features.. 49
8.3.4   Database-driven IETM Applications in the Occasionally
           Connected Mode 50

CONTENTS

PARAGRAPH   PAGE

8.3.4.1   Linking and Addressing 50
8.3.4.2   Multiple Database-driven IETMs... 50
8.3.5   Application Development Considerations 50
8.3.5.1   Custom Server-side Applications, Extensions, or Databases............ 50
8.3.5.2   Automated Replication of Databases 51
8.4   Stand-alone IETM Applications... 51
8.4.1   Web Server Support and Implementation... 51
8.4.1.1   Web Servers and Stand-alone Configurations 51
8.4.1.2   Stand-alone Configuration Features.. 52
8.4.2   Database-driven IETM Applications in the Stand-alone Mode........ 52
8.4.3   Application Development Considerations 53
8.4.3.1   Linking and Addressing 53
8.4.3.2   Multiple Database-driven IETMs... 53

9.0   MAINTAINING A COMMON LOOK AND FEEL AMONG
             DIFFERING IETMs.. 53
9.1   Joint DoD/industry User-Interaction Guidelines............................. 53
9.2   Preliminary User-Interaction Guidelines for DoD IETMs................ 54
9.2.1   Display Format (text/font, graphics, table, lists, object
             embedding)... 54
9.2.2   Browse Capability.. 54
9.2.3   Link Behavior/Navigation... 54
9.2.4   Control Bars 54
9.2.5   Icon Standardization.. 55
9.2.6   Selectable Elements (Hot Spots).. 56
9.2.7   Warnings, Cautions, Notes.. 56
9.2.8   Search & Lookup 56
9.2.9   Session Control (Suspend, Resume, Nested Sessions) 57
9.2.10   Context Filtering.. 57
9.2.11   Screen Resolution and Color Guidelines 57
9.2.12   Information Access (indices, Electronic TOCs, etc)......................... 57
9.2.13   Dialogs 58
9.2.14   Sound... 58
9.2.15   Voice Input/Output (I/O).. 58
9.2.16   Graphics 58
9.2.17   Hardware User Interface (e.g., Point and Click, Voice, Selection
             Keys, A/N Keyboard, Touch Pad, etc.).. 58
9.2.18   Performance (Response Time by Context) 58
9.2.19   Printer Output... 59
9.2.20   User Annotations (e.g., comments, user notes, redlines,
             bookmarks)... 59
9.2.21   Feedback to Originator (e.g., TMDRs, Form 2028, AFTO 22)........ 59

CONTENTS

PARAGRAPH   PAGE

9.2.22   Administrative Information (e.g., effectivity, authorization,
            distribution, validation/verification)... 60
9.2.23   Interface to External References and Systems............................... 60
9.2.24   Rapid Action Changes and Critical Safety Interim Messages 60
9.2.25   Major Data Types (e.g., troubleshooting, procedural, parts,
            descriptive).. 60

10.0   NOTES... 60
10.1   Intended Use.. 60
10.2   Subject Term (Keyword) Listing... 60

LIST OF FIGURES

FIGURES   PAGE

Figure 1   Flow of an IETM and the Information Access Processes
            in the JIA.. 12
Figure 2   IETM Architecture Building Block.. 23
Figure 3   Elements for Architecture Types C1 and C2 31
Figure 4   Elements for Architecture Types S1 32
Figure 5   Elements for Architecture Types S2 33
Figure 6   IETM Architecture Building Blocks.. 36
Figure 7   Illustration of the Key Parts of the JIA with Principle Web
            Server and Database Interface Components Identified...................... 44
Figure 8   Networked Client/Server IETM Applications................................. 46
Figure 9   Occasionally Connected Mode Applications 48
Figure 10   Stand-Alone IETM Applications 51

LIST OF TABLES

TABLE   PAGE

I   Target IETM Constituency...   2
II   IETM Architecture Types   29
III   IETM Entity Address Features and Benefits....................................   37
IV   External Entity Address Specifications..   37
V   vURL Structure Attributes...   38
VI   Guidance for Establishing vURLs in the JIA..................................   40
VII   IETM Component Registry Features/Benefits................................   43
VIII   IETM Component Registry Specifications   43

          INDEX   61

1.   SCOPE

1.1   Scope. The purpose of this handbook is to outline issues associated with achieving IETM interoperability through the use of a common user interface, i.e., a browser. Not all areas of interoperability, i.e., data interoperability are covered in this handbook. The guidance contained herein specifically covers issues that may allow an IETM user access to IETMs via a common interface regardless of where, by who, and how the IETM was created.

Note

Managers should acquire JIA-compliant IETMs only when:

(1) Cost Benefit Analyses or other similar "business case" tools have indicated the acquisition of JIA-compliant IETMs to be cost effective throughout the life of weapon system/equipment.

(2) Careful and comprehensive consultations with all intended users of the JIA-compliant IETMs indicate that the IETMs will be usable and sustainable in all of their operational environments.

(3) An adequate infrastructure is in place, in all operational environments, to allow the timely viewing and accessing JIA-compliant IETMs using web-based technologies such as a DoD Intranet.

(4) An Implementation Guide has been written to establish service-specific rules for implementation of the JIA.

1.2   Application. This Handbook applies to all Department of Defense (DOD) IETM acquisition and development activities. These activities can be divided into the following major constituencies:

 a. The preparers of the acquisition documents (e.g., TMCRs).

 b. The creators and developers of the IETMs.

 c. The developers of the IETM user-infrastructure for both the distribution infrastructure and the user-site intranet.

 d. The procurers of the common user display systems with the JIA-compliant browser software installed on these devices.

The following matrix highlights the relevance of the four proposed requirement areas (described in detail in the body of this document) to the four constituencies:

TABLE I. Target IETM Constituency

Requirement Area	Preparer of IETM Acquisition Documents	IETM Developer	Infrastructure Provider	User System Provider
Object Encapsulation & Component Interface	Cite along with general requirements of Sec 4.2 as primary requirement for IETM deliverable	Principal Requirement for IETM Form		
Server & Database Interface	Cite this requirement if IETM will employ Application Server or DBMS	Rules of Cooperation between IETM developer and Infrastructure when server extensions and/or a DBMS need to be installed as part of delivered IETM.		
Common Browser	Cite requirement that IETM must be viewable on any Browser that meets this requirement and that any plug-ins not referenced must be included with IETM deliverable.	Statement of the capability which can be assumed of user-system. i.e., any additional functionality must be provided as a software component in the IETM.	Utilize requirement when need to provide User Systems as part of infrastructure.	Statement of minimum capability to be met in procuring COTS systems.
Addressing Model and Library Index	Cite that content of IETM must conform to this Addressing and Library Index requirement.	Used as guide for preparing electronic address for references to other IETMs external to IETM being provided. Also contains requirement for index data (i.e., metadata) format.	Should provide for server remapping and Domain Name Services (DNS). Format of metadata available for index server.	

This Handbook will also provide additional guidance to the Program Manager's staff in preparing the needed IETM-acquisition documents. Table I above provides some guidance to these personnel, who might not otherwise be aware of their role in implementing the JIA.

1.3   Background. In 1992 the DoD issued several Military Specifications for service-wide use in the acquisition of IETMs that are now being acquired for many of the DoD's major weapon systems. The individual services have noticed substantial incompatibility between many of these IETM systems and the growing inventory of legacy-data Electronic Technical Manual (ETM) systems (to which the Specifications were not directed). The result has been that although authoring systems and the presentation systems developed for an individual IETM were interdependent, they were incompatible with other IETM or legacy-based ETM systems. An IETM authored by one activity usually could not be viewed using a presentation system developed by another activity, nor could it electronically reference or incorporate the legacy-ETM information when needed to support the Technical Information. As the use of IETMs became more widespread, and as IETMs were deployed at multiple sites, it became more important to establish a consistent infrastructure to manage and distribute IETM updates to the field sites and to provide life-cycle support for the numerous types of IETMs. In this environment, the fact that differing IETMs cannot interoperate (i.e., cannot be viewed on the same standard presentation system, or electronically reference each other to any meaningful level of internal granularity) is a major impediment.

1.3.1 <u>Tri-Service Approach to Solving the Problem</u>. Starting in 1997, the DoD Tri-Service IETM Technology Working Group (IETMTWG), then chartered by the OSD CALS Office of DUSD(L), sponsored a DoD-wide study based on an earlier Navy project, which developed a Navy IETM Architecture (NIA). At the request of the OSD CALS Office, the IETMTWG expanded the Navy study into a DoD-wide effort that involved modifying, prototyping, and testing a version of the Navy-initiated interoperability methodology which could be applicable to all of the services. At the same time, the proposed IETMTWG plan was presented to the Technical Publications Sub-panel of the Joint [Logistics] Commanders Group for Communications and Electronics (JCG-CE) as a means of meeting some of the major goals of the JCG-CE Publications Panel. These goals included the achievement of field interoperability for IETMs. The proposed approach was approved and the JLC recommended, by a memorandum of 10 June 1997, that the OSD CALS Office implement this plan as a joint effort of the JCG-CE and the IETMTWG. This DoD-wide effort technically started in late 1997 and continued through September 1999. The OSD CALS office has since been reorganized as DUSD(L)/LRO (Logistics Reinvention Office of the Office of the Deputy Undersecretary of Defense for Logistics), which is currently the chartering activity for the IETMTWG and the sponsor of this JIA Task with funding coming from the Joint Electronic Commerce Project Office (JECPO).

1.3.2 <u>Objective and Primary Goal for the Architecture</u>. The objective for the JIA is to establish an architectural framework for acquisition and deployment of the whole spectrum of Electronic Technical Manuals. The objective is that when the sharable and interoperable technical information is distributed to the work location of end-users, they can view and utilize that data through a common user interface, no matter what the authoring source or data format. To obtain this objective, the overall approach for JIA development has been to base it on the use of existing COTS (Commercial-Off-The-Shelf) Internet and World-Wide-Web technology. The JIA is not a new or even a redesigned technical architecture. It is the architecture of the Internet and the World Wide Web, profiled for DoD IETMs and implemented on secure DoD intranets. It is primarily a reference vehicle for shifting the inventory of DoD IETMs to a form and format suitable for long-term use on the Defense Information Infrastructure (DII), as it emerges and is available for the distribution and use of maintenance and job-aiding information.

The primary goal of the JIA is to achieve end-user-level interoperability of the IETMs delivered to and used by the entire DoD Operational Community. In this context, an ETM or IETM is defined as having end-user interoperability when it can enable a user with one common, commercially available display device, such as a portable personal computer:

a. To view and interact with Technical Information from any source and of any internal format; and

b. To automatically access and view, by means of an electronic-link reference in the displayed Technical Information, additional information in any other ETM or IETM with which the link connects him.

The JIA has been developed to provide interoperability for all levels of Electronic Technical Manuals including all five established DoD IETM Classes from the digitized page-oriented Electronic Technical Manuals to the highly integrated Interactive Electronic Technical Manuals.

2.   APPLICABLE DOCUMENTS

2.1   <u>General</u>. The documents listed below are not necessarily all of the documents referenced herein, but are the ones that are needed in order to fully understand the information provided by this handbook.

2.2   <u>Government Documents</u>.

2.2.1   <u>Specifications, Standards, and Handbooks</u>. The following specifications, standards, and handbooks form a part of this document to the extent specified herein. Unless otherwise specified, the issues of these documents are those listed in the latest issue of the Department of Defense Index of Specifications and Standards (DoDISS), and supplements thereto, and are referenced for guidance only.

SPECIFICATIONS

MIL-PRF-87268	Manuals, Interactive Electronic Technical: General Content, Style, Format, and User-Interaction

STANDARDS

FIPS 140-1	Security Requirements for Cryptic Modules
MIL-STD-1808	System Subsystem Sub-subsystem Numbering
MIL-STD-38784	Manuals, Technical: General Style and Format Requirements

HANDBOOKS

(Unless otherwise indicated, copies of the above specifications, standards, and handbooks are available from the Standardization Document Order Desk, 700 Robbins Avenue, Building 4D, Philadelphia, PA 19111.)

2.3   Non-Government Publications. The following documents form a part of this document to the extent specified herein. Unless otherwise specified, the issues of the documents that are Department of Defense (DoD) adopted are those listed in the latest issue of the DoDISS, and supplement thereto.

> AECMA 1000D   International Specification for Technical Data Publications, Utilizing a Common Source Data Base

(Copies of AECMA 1000D may be ordered from the following website: http:\\www.aecma.org\publish.htm.)

2.4   Order of Precedence. In the event of a conflict between the text of this document and the references cited herein, the text of this document takes precedence. Nothing in this document, however, supersedes applicable laws and regulations unless a specific exemption has been obtained.

3.   DEFINITIONS

3.1   Acronyms Used in this Handbook. The acronyms used in this handbook are defined as follows:

AECMA	Association Européenne des Constructeurs de Materiel Aerospatial
AFTO	Air Force Technical Order
AIFF	Audio Interchange File Format
APL	Allowable Parts Lists
ASP	Active Server Page
ATIS	Advanced Technical Information Support
AVI	AudioVisual Interface
CAGE	Commercial and Government Entity
CALS	Continuous Acquisition and Life-cycle Support
CD-ROM	Compact Disk - Read Only Memory
CERN	European Laboratory for Particle Physics
CGI	Common Gateway Interface
CGM	Computer Graphics Metafile
COE	Common Operating Environment
COM	Component Object Model
COMSEC	Communication Security
CORBA	Common Object Request Broker Architecture
COTS	Commercial Off-the-Shelf
CSS	Cascading Style Sheets
DBMS	Database Management System
DCOM	Distributed Component Object Model
DII	Defense Information Infrastructure
DISA	Defense Information Standardization Agency
DNS	Domain Name Service

DoD	Department of Defense
DoDISS	Department of Defense Index of Specifications and Standards
DTD	Document Type Definition
DUSD(L)	(Office of the) Deputy Undersecretary of Defense for Logistics
DVD-ROM	Digital Video/Versatile Disk - Read Only Memory
ECP	Engineering Change Proposal
EIC	Equipment Identification Code
EPS	Encapsulated Postscript
ETM	Electronic Technical Manual
FIPS	Federal Information Processing Standard
FTP	File Transfer Protocol
GCSS	Global Combat Support System
GI	Generic Identifier
HTML	HyperText Markup Language
HTTP	HyperText Transport Protocol
IETF	Internet Engineering Task Force
IETM	Interactive Electronic Technical Manual
IETMTWG	IETM Technology Working Group
ILSP	Integrated Logistics Support Plan
I/O	Input/Output
IP	Internet Protocol
IPB	Illustrated Parts Breakdown
IRAC	Interim Rapid Action Change
ISAPI	Internet Information Server Application Programming Interface
ISO	International Organization for Standardizatio
JCG	Joint [Logistics] Commander's Group for Communications and Electronics
JECPO	Joint Electronic Commerce Project Office
JEDMICS	Joint Engineering Data Management Information and Control System
JIA	Joint IETM Architecture
JIT	Just In Time
JLC	Joint Logistics Commanders
JPEG	Joint Photographic Experts Group
JTA	Joint Technical Architecture
LAN	Local Area Network
LOGSA	Logistics Support Activity
LRO	Logistics Reinvention Office
NATO	North Atlantic Treaty Organization
NIA	Navy IETM Architecture
NIIN	National Item Identification Number
NIST	National Institute of Standards and Technology
NSAPI	Netscape Server Application Programming Interface
NSN	National Stock Number
OSD	Office of the Secretary of Defense
PDF	Portable Document Format

PEDD	Portable Electronic Display Device
PKI	Public Key Infrastructure
PNG	Portable Network Graphic
PPPI	Pre-Planned Product Improvement
RAC	Rapid Action Change
RDF	Resource Description Framework
RFC	Request For Comment
RPSTL	Repair Parts and Special Tools List
SGML	Standard Generalized Markup Language
SQL	Structured Query Language
SSI	Server Side Include
SSL	Secure Socket Layer
SSSN	System Subsystem Sub-subsystem Numbering
TCP	Transmission Control Protocol
TEI	Text Encoding Initiative
TIFF	Tagged Image File Format
TM	Technical Manual
TMCR	Technical Manual Contract Requirement
TMSS	Technical Manuals Specifications and Standards
TO	Technical Order
TOC	Table of Contents
URI	Uniform Resource Identifier
URL	Uniform Resource Locator
VBS	Visual Basic Script
VP	View Package
VRML	Virtual Reality Modeling Language
vURL	virtual Uniform Resource Locator
WAV	(Windows standard for) Waveform Sound Files
W3C	World Wide Web Consortium
WWW	World Wide Web
XLL	XML Linking Language
XML	eXtensible Markup Language
XSL	eXtensible Style Language

3.2   Definitions of Selected Terms.

3.2.1   Distribution Code. One of the following statements which indicates to whom the document can be given:

a. Statement A - Approved for public release; distribution is unlimited.

b. Statement B - Distribution authorized to U.S. Government agencies only.

c. Statement C - Distribution authorized to U.S. Government agencies and their contractors only.

d. Statement D - Distribution authorized to the Department of Defense (DoD) and DoD contractors only.

e. Statement E - Distribution authorized to DoD components only.

f. Statement F - Further dissemination only as directed by proponent or higher authority.

g. Statement X - Distribution authorized to U.S. Government agencies and private individuals or enterprises eligible to obtain export-controlled technical data in accordance with regulations implementing 10 USC 130C.

3.2.2   Element. Each eXtensible Markup Language (XML) document contains one or more *elements*, the boundaries of which are either delimited by *start-tags* and *end-tags*, or for *empty* elements by an empty-element tag. Each element has a type, identified by name, sometimes called its "Generic Identifier" (GI), and may have a set of attribute specifications. Each attribute specification has a *name* and a *value*.

3.2.3   End Item. A final combination of end articles, component parts and materials that are ready for its intended use (e.g., ship, tank, mobile machine shop, aircraft, receiver, rifle, or recorder).

3.2.4   End-User Interoperability. The ability of an IETM user access to IETMs via a common interface regardless of where, by who, and how the IETM was created.

3.2.5   Entity (SGML/XML). An XML document may consist of one or many virtual storage units. These are called *entities*; they all have content and are all (except for the document entity, see below, and the external Document Type Definition (DTD) subset) identified by *name*. Each XML document has one entity called the document entity, which serves as the starting point for the XML processor and may contain the whole document.

3.2.6   External Entity (SGML/XML). A resource that resides in a separate storage object from the referencing entity. An entity contains one or more IETM components.

3.2.7   IETM Component. A reusable entity that is used to instantiate an entire technical manual (or Technical Order) or an identifiable element (that may be defined by a DTD) within the structure of a technical manual (e.g., a maintenance or inspection procedure, illustration, work package, chapter, section, appendix). See Logical Object definition.

3.2.8   Inline Link. Abstractly, a link which serves as one of its own resources. Concretely, a link where the content of the linking element serves as a participating resource. HTML A, HyTime clink (contextual link), and Text Encoding Initiative (TEI) XREF are all examples of inline links.

3.2.9 <u>Link</u>. An explicit relationship between two or more data objects or portions of data objects.

3.2.10 <u>Linking Elements</u>. An element that asserts the existence and describes the characteristics of a link.

3.2.11 <u>Locator</u>. Data, provided as part of a link, which identifies a resource.

3.2.12 <u>Logical Object</u>. A logical object is: an IETM; a Work Package (Actions, Parts, Other elements); a maintenance, operational, or inspection or other procedure; or Informational Object (e.g., Warnings, Cautions, Notes).

3.2.13 <u>Metadata</u>. Data about data. Describes how and when and by whom a particular set of data was collected and how the data is formatted.

3.2.14 <u>NSN</u>. The 13-digit NSN consisting of the four-digit Federal Supply Classification Code and the nine-digit National Item Identification Number (NIIN). The NIIN consists of a two-digit National Codification Bureau Code designating the cataloging office of the North Atlantic Treaty Organization (NATO) or other friendly country that assigned the number, and a seven-digit (XXX-XXXX) non-significant number. The NSNs should be listed in consecutive numerical sequence.

3.2.15 <u>Out-of-Line Link</u>. A link whose content does not serve as one of the link's participating resources. Such links presuppose a notion like extended link groups, which indicate to application software where to look for links. Out-of-line links are generally needed for supporting multidirectional traversal and for allowing read-only resources to have outgoing links.

3.2.16 <u>Resource</u>. In the abstract sense, an addressable unit of information or service that is participating in a link. Examples include files, images, documents, programs, and query results. Concretely, anything reachable by the use of a locator in some linking element. Note that this term and its definition are taken from the basic specifications governing the World Wide Web (WWW).

3.2.17 <u>Technical Manual (TM)</u>. A publication that contains instructions for the installation, operation, maintenance, training and support of weapon systems, weapon system components, support equipment and other items procured for the DoD. TM information may be presented in any form or characteristic, including, but not limited to, hard copy, audio and visual displays, magnetic tape, discs, and other electronic devices. A TM normally includes operational and maintenance instructions, parts lists, or parts breakdown, and related technical information exclusive of administrative procedures. Technical Orders (TOs) that meet the criteria of this definition may also be classified as TMs.

3.2.18 <u>Uniform Resource Identifier</u>. A URI is a compact string of characters for identifying an abstract or physical resource.

3.2.19 <u>View Package</u>. The data and the viewing software bundled and shipped together.

3.2.20 <u>Virtual Uniform Resource Locator (vURL)</u>. A proposed naming scheme for IETM resources that use indirect addressing to minimize software maintenance of calling IETMs.

4. GENERAL GUIDANCE

4.1 <u>Overview of the Joint IETM Architecture</u>. The Joint IETM Architecture (JIA) is firmly based on the proven and widely accepted Internet and World Wide Web technology, but is directed at implementations on private, contained, and controlled DoD intranets. Such intranets can be configured as a private DoD World-wide network, as a combat-capable unit-wide local intranet, or simply as a group of computers in close proximity, hard-wired in a local Ethernet configuration. They can also be configured as a single display device (portable or workstation personal computer) which operates as both an IETM browser and a personal single-user Web server. The technology for implementing such intranets is low-risk, easily implemented, and widely understood by the IETM-software community. The proposed Architecture is based entirely on the commercial standards and Commercial Off-the-Shelf (COTS) technology being made available for use on the World Wide Web. A dedicated intranet constituting a JIA IETM implementation is composed of Web browsers, Web servers, and a network to connect them if they are not contained in the same computer. An IETM implementation on an intranet may also include other optional Database Servers and Application Servers in addition to the principal HyperText Transport Protocol (HTTP) Web-servers.

4.1.1 <u>Overall Joint IETM Architecture Concept</u>. The overall concept of the JIA is to utilize the group of emerging technologies that the commercial marketplace is rapidly adopting as the standard for distributable electronic documents. These, in general, are based on the technology of the Internet and the World Wide Web. For security and operational reasons, the JIA is not intended to utilize the actual public Internet or the World Wide Web itself, but may employ essentially the same technology and COTS products in a private and dedicated DoD intranet environment. A major objective of the JIA is to achieve end-user interoperability of both proprietary and legacy IETMs. This should be accomplished by encapsulating or packaging them into a common view package (VP) (the name given to the encapsulated object of the IETM) format, which can be electronically distributed to DoD intranets and eventually viewed by an end-user employing a single user-information interface (i.e., a Web browser). This process is referred to herein as "object encapsulation;" that is, the process of "object encapsulation" creates a valuable IETM View Package. Such a capability may need the employment of the following technical capabilities:

   a. An authoring framework which (regardless of which authoring tools are used) can effectively create and manage IETM source data and subsequently create interoperable IETM view packages for delivery to the Government distribution and user activities;

b. An infrastructure that permits a military agency to distribute, manage, and deliver these IETM view packages; and

c. A viewing system and a methodology for the end-user to access and view the necessary technical information, and to retrieve relevant data from other IETMs, including those of other Services, as necessary.

In order to achieve interoperability, the interface recommendations while specific, are constructed so as to encourage innovative and effective solutions, especially in light of the constantly expanding technology base of the commercial environment. Achieving this balance has created some decisions that may need to be reexamined over time. However, whenever possible, the design should conform to open standards and/or de facto Internet standards widely implemented by multiple vendors, with the clear intent to maximize the use of commercially available software products. Figure 1 shows the flow of an IETM and the associated information access processes in a typical implementation of the JIA. It illustrates the employment of the JIA by the original IETM developer, the management infrastructure repository, the user-site intranet server, and the end-user who selects the next object to view via a point-and-click Web-browser interface. The "Presentation component" referred to in Figure 1 can be a client or a server software component that is either delivered with the IETM content or assumed to be preinstalled in the browser, in which case it is "implied" and not included in the delivered package.

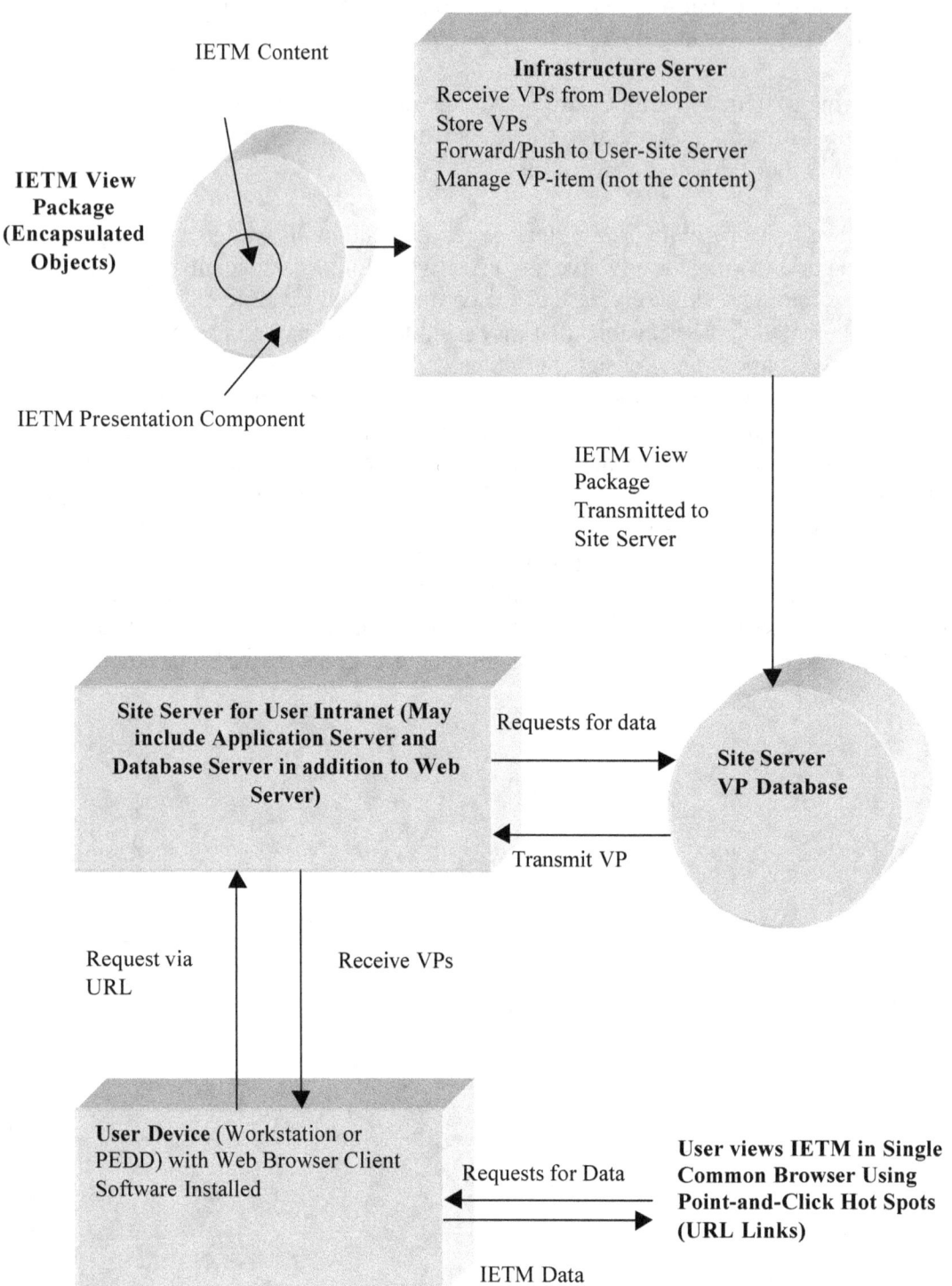

IETM Content

Infrastructure Server
Receive VPs from Developer
Store VPs
Forward/Push to User-Site Server
Manage VP-item (not the content)

IETM View
Package
(Encapsulated
Objects)

IETM Presentation Component

IETM View
Package
Transmitted to
Site Server

Site Server for User Intranet (May
include Application Server and
Database Server in addition to Web
Server)

Requests for data

Site Server
VP Database

Transmit VP

Request via
URL

Receive VPs

User Device (Workstation or
PEDD) with Web Browser Client
Software Installed

Requests for Data

User views IETM in Single
Common Browser Using
Point-and-Click Hot Spots
(URL Links)

IETM Data

FIGURE 1. Flow of an IETM and the Information Access Processes in the JIA

4.1.2 <u>Basic Architecture Independent of Operating System.</u> The basic architecture is not intended for, nor constrained to, any specific operating system or combinations of operating systems. Individual services or programs may restrict their IETM applications to a single operating environment, but the JIA does not require a specific operating system. The JIA is intentionally flexible in this regard. In some cases a weapon-specific feature or functionality may need advanced functionality (e.g., downloadable diagnostic components contain active agents for collection of on-board data) that operate only with a specific operating environment and thus not be fully interoperable. However, some limited universal availability can exist in that such an application can still be hosted and made available on a general-purpose JIA-compliant intranet since the Web-based network concept, upon which the JIA is based, can easily host multiple operating systems for the various Client and Server computers.

4.1.3 <u>Developing a Solution for IETM Interoperability.</u> The approach to developing a solution for the problem of interoperability among IETMs from various sources has been to adapt commercial and industry applications involving electronic documentation for which there is widespread vendor-product support and these are essentially all Web-based products to some degree. Taking into account the rapid changes that have been occurring in Internet technology, the JIA has been designed to be extensible, flexible, and able to accommodate the predictable rapid growth in technology for all aspects of the Internet, the Web, and the emerging electronic-documentation applications being developed to operate on the Web. Updates to any guidance document for the acquisition of JIA-compliant IETMs should be based on a continuing study of emerging military requirements and compared with the current state of commercial technology and available COTS products to assure that they still met the DoD requirements in the future. The primary areas relating to the JIA in which the needs of the military and commercial communities may differ are those involving communication security (COMSEC) and information assurance, and the overall administratively imposed requirements for operational presence on the DII (e.g., operating system limitations, restrictions on use of downloadable components, etc.).

4.2 <u>Characteristics of the Architecture Which Should Be Preserved in Future JIA Implementations.</u> Certain characteristics detailed herein are expected to be rendered obsolete by events and/or emerging-technologies. In such cases, developers and their DoD customers may need to refine and update some of these technical recommendations. The non-technical functional and operational characteristics described in 4.2.1 through 4.2.3 should be preserved even as specific recommendations are modified and updated by technological progress.

4.2.1 <u>Characteristics of the JIA for the User.</u> The following functional and operational characteristics should be preserved for the user.

a. The principal characteristic of the JIA for the user is that it enables an end-user with a single display device and a single graphic user interface (i.e., a Web browser) to read and utilize any DoD IETM accessible to that device, no matter which Service or Program originated the IETM. In performing an assigned task, the user should access and view the IETMs with either a workstation personal computer in a shop environment or a Portable Electronic Display Device (PEDD). The portable device can be configured either as a network client attached to the operational unit intranet or it can be reconfigured to operate in stand-alone or detached mode. In either case, the user cannot determine from the look-and-feel of a screen display the mode in which the device is operating.

b. The major effect of the JIA on the user is that all technical information is viewed through a common (i.e., single) and very familiar Web browser interface. The JIA conforming IETMs should avoid externally launched viewing applications (typically called "helper applications") which are not managed (i.e., structurally closed after use) by the browser and employ the use of plug-ins instead. The IETM may launch another browser session as long as the session is controlled by the launching browser window. To access an IETM, the user selects a URL (Uniform Resource Locator; the form of electronic address used by the World Wide Web) using one of the many access-screen or menu-select options available. Selection options include such approaches as a Windows favorites list, explicit entries in a predefined pick list, a pre-assembled list of active IETMs on a squadron "Home Page," a hot-spotted index graphic, or a standard job-assignment form listing needed technical references as hot spots. An important characteristic of the JIA is that all of these features are common practices borrowed directly from the World Wide Web community. From the user's perspective, the referenced IETM content simply appears next in the display-device's browser window. When it is necessary to utilize a specific viewer plug-in for a standard data type, for which there exist multiple viewers (e.g., CGM, TIFF), the IETM should provide a mechanism for specifying and utilizing a specific plug-in at view-time for that particular data type. The user should get the same look and feel (i.e., format of the particular software package) of the displayed graphic every time, even if different viewing devices are utilized.

c. All recommended browser software components are automatically loaded (i.e., installed) into the browser with minimal user involvement. A major benefit to the user organization is that no explicit software installations are needed to utilize an IETM, even with a device employing a brand new "out-of-the-box" JIA-conforming browser. Depending on the established browser security level, the user may, at times, need to explicitly accept software components that need installation, by a single-click acknowledgment. Other than that action, no explicit installation action should be needed because the browser installs the components automatically. This is an essential user-friendly feature of the JIA and should eliminate the need for a trained and certified system administrator to install user software. This feature is part of the simplicity of the JIA approach and one of the largest potential cost savers.

Note

However, there is a security concern with such downloaded components that should be balanced with the benefits. These software components can host destructive viruses and other malevolent software code. Because of this threat, the DOD may impose restrictions and constraints on the use of what is being called "Mobile Code" and these policies should be observed in developing and fielding IETMs. The specifics of such policies are not known at this time, but they may involve such factors as restricting the use of Active-X and some Java Script, effectively needing more server hosting for the general situation and the use of specific actions to take when downloading components such as an extra filter process for virus checking.

d. The primary user interface is the "point-and-click" methodology. If one IETM contains a reference to another IETM, the user should be able to "click on" the highlighted reference and the referenced IETM should automatically appear in a browser window (assuming, of course, the referenced IETM exists on the user's intranet). This display can be either the same browser window replacing the referencing information, or a secondary browser session that is under the control of the calling instance (i.e., the calling instance should be able to close the secondary browser window). This second IETM can, in turn, reference a third IETM, etc. To return to the original IETM, the user can simply use the "Back" arrow on the browser interface, effectively reversing the sequence of references. An important characteristic of such browser management is that the browser manages the software and data components utilized along the way. The user need not launch or close out application software. Success in this area is measured by the extent to which the user is not aware that a browser-managed system-clean-up action is going on. Modern Web browsers can handle many levels of such nested referencing with no performance degradation, a very powerful feature. The JIA is intended to make the use of disparate IETMs as easy and "seamless" as possible by use of modern technology. Because of the nature of the Web-browser technology employed, the user should experience a great deal of common "look-and-feel" in the interactive (navigation-control) area, even if the individual IETM user-interface for the content varies.

e. JIA implementations should also facilitate a common practice on the World Wide Web of employing search engines for accessing IETMs such as those employed by the well-known companies Yahoo and Excite. The JIA Library Model and the recommended standard HyperText Markup Language/eXtensible Markup Language (HTML/XML)-encoded metadata package are specifically designed to facilitate the inclusion of search engines on a JIA-conforming intranet. In these search engines, the user enter's a "string" or list of key word(s) or reference designator(s), and the search engine identifies IETM references available on the user's intranet. The JIA does not specify a specific search engine, but a rich selection of commercially available search engines build their indices from XML- and HTML-encoded sources and can easily be employed on a JIA intranet. However, such a capability serves users better on the connected network as not all of the commercially available search engines support the detached or stand-alone operational environments. The ability to get all the information needed to perform a task in a timely and convenient manner has been, from the beginning of the IETM concept, one of the important performance-enhancing capabilities of IETMs. This JIA implementation, using low cost commercially available technology, should permit even greater capability in this area.

4.2.2 <u>Characteristics of the JIA to be Maintained by the IETM Developer</u>. The following characteristics should be preserved by the IETM developer when developing IETMs for DoD use.

a. All software components and data needed to make an IETM accessible on the JIA display device are packaged into a single digital product (i.e., the encapsulated objects). The encapsulated objects can be easily combined and installed as a set of data files (a view package) onto an intranet-server file system and subsequently automatically delivered to the user as the IETM is accessed. There should be no additional separate path for this delivery and installation of user software other than the primary delivery path for the encapsulated object.

b. Object-oriented methodology recommended by the JIA is a primary benefit to the IETM developer in that the developer is free to choose whatever authoring and development environment he prefers. The JIA does not dictate how the IETM is to be developed nor what the internal format of the IETM object should be. The external interfaces are specified, but they are in accordance with most of the modern electronic-document authoring environments that are rapidly being adapted to operate on the World Wide Web and, as such, should operate equally well on a JIA-compliant intranet. Additionally, it is easy to test most aspects of JIA compliance at the contractor's site, in that proofing tools for the IETM objects are also easy to set up in the developer's facility. It may also be possible to validate other aspects of the IETM, such as the actual information content, on such a test network without utilizing a military environment; however, these factors are out of scope for this Handbook. The JIA browsers are made up of readily available software products, which the authoring activity can easily procure without going through DoD supply channels. The design philosophy for the JIA is to use the best readily available commercial practices for developing and deploying IETM products.

c. While the technology needed to bundle all of the IETM components into a single digital package is complex, it is readily available in off-the-shelf COTS Web-based software products. A foundational principal of the JIA is that the products developed for the Internet can be used unmodified to develop IETM products for a JIA-compliant intranet.

4.2.3 <u>Characteristics of the JIA for the DoD IETM Distribution Infrastructure</u>. The following characteristics should be preserved for the DoD IETM distribution infrastructure.

a. Encapsulated IETM view packages can be distributed without requiring that the distributing system "know" what is inside the electronic capsules. The infrastructure activities can, therefore, consist simply of electronic-package distribution centers, for which the DoD has substantial experience, and not data-processing centers, which are much more difficult to operate and staff.

b. Within the JIA, a complete set of IETM-content and associated presentation components (see Figure 1) is called an IETM view package. All view package delivery to the end-user network is accomplished through standard Web-based interaction. A feature of this concept is that the view package can be passed, unmodified, from server to server as part of the JIA electronic-distribution system. The key JIA concept for creation and use of the infrastructure server is that the IETM view packages are composed of self-contained digital objects that appear to the infrastructure simply as large standard binary-formatted digital files. These files can easily be transferred over any intranet, using common File Transfer Protocol (FTP) processes or transmitted on a common Compact Disk-Read Only Memory (CD-ROM). A View Package can be received from a developer, stored, forwarded, and delivered from one server to another without any need for the infrastructure agents to know the internal structure of the View Package itself. Thus, the infrastructure site can function more as a supply center than as an information-systems center.

c. In order for the JIA to assure meaningful interoperability over time, a high priority function of the permanent IETM infrastructure should be to preserve and publish the IETM addressing registries (discussed in section 7 of this Handbook). These registries are needed for users to be able to locate and access referenced IETMs, for intranet implementers to be able to manage the JIA addressing mechanism, and for IETM developers/authors to be able to determine which electronic addresses to use in their IETM when referencing external IETMs. All of these communities need confidence that this registry is current, permanent, stable, and should be maintained over time.

Note

The specific design and development of any specific DoD or service infrastructure was not in the scope of the JIA effort itself. Such an infrastructure design is undoubtedly complex, difficult, but important task that is complicated by the impact it has on many existing DoD and commercial business practices. However, this key JIA element, which enables the IETM view packages to be processed as an item of supply (with no requirement to manage the internal content or structure of the object), should make this task much more manageable.

4.3   Summary of Recommendations for Implementation of the Joint IETM Architecture. In addition to using the de facto standards of the Word Wide Web, such as the HTTP, FTP, and TCP/IP networking protocols utilized by the Internet and by virtually all commercial Web-based intranet products and COTS systems, the JIA has specific functional and interface recommendations in four areas, which are presented in detail in Sections 4 through 8 of this Handbook. These are: (1) Common Browser, (2) Object Encapsulation and Component Interface, (3) Electronic-Addressing and Library Functions, and (4) Intranet Server and Database Interface. Performance criteria is needed in all of these areas to guide the process of attaining and providing for the interoperability to view and access disparate IETMs by the end-user.

4.3.1   Common Browser. The need for a common browser applies to the user of a Portable Electronic Delivery Devices (PEDDs) and individual workstations, since installation of a standard browser is needed for these devices. A browser software component, which is not included in the IETM view package, should be pre-installed on the user device. However, the providers of the IETM should also be aware of the details of this minimal recommendation since their IETM should be developed in such a manner that it can be viewed using a JIA-compliant browser not provided by the IETM developer. A usable IETM cannot exist without a browser, of course, because a browser is essential for IETM access; however, the exact version of the browser varies from user device to user device. Additionally, the minimum configuration of the browser may necessitate some extensions to the commercially released products. This can be made via specified plug-ins; e.g., viewing capabilities common in military IETMs, but not in the general marketplace, such as Computer Graphics Metafile (CGM) or the common Portable Document Format (PDF) used for legacy TMs. Additionally, the JIA recommends support for XML, HTML 4.0 with CSS-2 support. The experience of the World Wide Web has demonstrated that such a concept is viable and the available of the more capable browser needed for JIA support will, in the future, be no great problem: such a basic browser capability is expected to be available on virtually any general-purpose single user COTS computer device available from commercial sources.

Refer to section 5 for a detailed description of the common browser recommendations.

4.3.2   Object Encapsulation and Component Interface.   A definition is needed for the delivery, transport, and structure of the integrated collection of software components and data contained in the IETM View Packages. In addition to IETM content and presentation components, the encapsulated object should include interfaces between multiple components when they exist, and the automated mechanisms for placing the IETM on the targeted intranet. It should also include the capability to automatically install these components on a presentation device in a manner sufficiently simple so that no professional system administrator is needed at the user site. From an architectural viewpoint, actual Object Encapsulation can be ordered so as to either operate at the user workstation (i.e., using the client software) or at the server installation. Refer to section 6 for a detailed description of the JIA Object Encapsulation process. Four Architectural Types, two client-centered and two server-centered, are designated respectively as C1, C2, S1, and S2, and are also described in section 6. Any of these types (or a combination thereof) is an allowable Object Encapsulation approach under the JIA. This Object Encapsulation recommendation constitutes the primary guidance needed to document to the IETM developer in what logical form the DoD customer needs the IETM View Package be prepared and delivered to the Government.

4.3.3   Electronic Addressing and Library Functions.

        a. Electronic addressing and library functions are the items that hold the collection of IETM information together by means of digitally encoded and executable-link references. This functionality itself defines the syntax and mechanism for building and executing the automated links to the IETM content and the IETM presentation software. Two additional areas regarding administration and enforcement of the recommendations are needed so that the enterprise-wide addressing concept works. The Electronic Addressing and Library Model functions may define these aspects, which may include the administration and allocation of the DoD-wide IETM "address space," the actual indexing or URL-based electronically-processible numbering system to which all the services and their suppliers should subscribe. The functionality also discusses the important area of the library model or the search-and-access mechanism, which can be used to perform an intelligent content-based access to another IETM when the exact specific locator (i.e., a URL) is not known. To support the proposed library-search functionality, the recommendations should also specify metadata files (encoded within a 'meta' tag in HTML or XML, e.g., serial number, version number, etc.), that serves as the primary searchable indices associated with each IETM.

        b. A specific technical and administrative impact in any real implementation of this addressing model is that the JIA utilizes a concept of virtual URLs. This imposition on the infrastructure to process the associated Domain Name Service (DNS) to assign the virtual URLs in an IETM to a specific server on which the referenced IETM is located, this in terms of its network address on the intranet being utilized. This is not a technically difficult issue because some DNS is needed for any intranet to operate. However, there may be an additional IETM-related administrative burden to add an additional IETM specific DNS to an existing network to execute JIA compliant IETMs. This is described in more detail in section 7.

4.3.4 <u>Intranet Server and Database Server Interface</u>. For those IETMs that need the services of both an intranet server and a user-site database server, the IETM supplier should provide the proper software extensions to the basic JIA intranet Web-server for access to the database server if they are not already in place. There is a need for cooperation between the constructors of the end-user intranet infrastructure and the IETM provider, who, in turn, need to establish the interfaces and protocols involved. The JIA is designed to recognize the fact that, in most cases, it is necessary to install software using conventional system-administration practices on fielded servers in order to achieve needed functionality. This also applies to server functionality in a stand-alone and/or "occasionally connected" application.

Note

This is not the case for the components fielded on JIA-conforming user browsers.

The guidance provided in section 8 documents the recommendations that an IETM provider should take into account when proposing or delivering such a capability for a JIA intranet.

4.4 <u>Communications Security and Information Assurance Recommendations</u>.

a. All IETMs developed to be JIA compliant should be designed to be usable within the Defense Information Infrastructure (DII) as it matures and becomes more available for logistics support operations. The functional area of using and deploying IETMs in the field is one of these logistics support areas and forms a part of what is being called the Global Combat Support System (GCSS). As such, the IETM applications will inherit the requirements for applications on the GCSS especially in the communications security and information assurance area. These apply to unclassified IETMs as well as classified IETMs. Requirements for classified DoD IETMs are not covered in this handbook.

b. IETMs should be conforming to the prescribed rules on communications security; however, it is likely that most of the specific IETM requirements and those of the associated infrastructure implementation apply to the network elements (i.e., browser implementation and settings, and Web servers) and not to the specific IETM view package itself. The communication and information-assurance security should involve user and server authentication and be layered around the IETM accessing and viewing processes, and should not be part of the IETM-specific view packages or the actual implementation. The principal exception to this statement is that the downloadable software components involved in an IETM (including diagnostic routines and software agents) should be digitally signed and issued a certificate by one of the official IETM management activities. These activities would be the same activities that would authorize or issue the IETM Virtual Uniform Resource Locators (vURLs) referred to in the Addressing Model recommendations discussed in section 7. It is, however, very clear that in accordance with emerging DoD policy (COMSEC references), any security mechanism implemented in any DoD IETM should be limited to those that employ only the certificates issued by the official DoD Public Key Infrastructure (PKI). In other words, proprietary or any other non-DoD security methodologies, no matter how much sense they make, should not be used if they in any way need the administration of a certificate (i.e., digital key) program which provides unique (i.e., other that the official DoD PKI issued) certificates to users.

4.5   Permitting IETM Use in a Stand-alone Environment. A typical military JIA intranet should have the capability of operating PEDDs (or other portable display devices) as stand-alone devices. Portable devices are more likely to be disconnected from any network during the time when an IETM is actually being viewed in support of a maintenance task. In many cases the portable user device is connected to the intranet network only occasionally, for the purpose of receiving needed information or for purposes of configuration management. This involve's the downloading of new or updated information, as well as the uploading of feedback reports, the ordering of parts, and the reporting of other logistics information.

4.5.1   Occasionally-Connected User Devices. It should be possible to carry out all the functionality of a distributed intranet, using a single device, by installing a personal Web-type server on the portable device. For advanced IETMs, additional servers that may be needed should be able to be installed. For some database-oriented IETM applications, a database management system (DBMS) which performs the database server function should be installed on the portable device, when the device is used in a stand-alone mode. In addition, configuration management should be built into the downloading system that is supplying data to the portable user devices. It should be possible to access any object loaded onto the portable device in exactly the same fashion as from the site server.

4.5.2   Dual-Mode IETMs. Two options should be considered for viewing IETMs in a stand-alone environment that does not require the installation of a Web server on the stand-alone, portable device. For either option, individual services may sponsor dual-use implementations of some IETMs, utilizing a stand-alone version for primary service use, and at the same time maintaining the option to incorporate the IETM unmodified in a JIA-compliant intranet with little or no additional effort. The two options are described below.

a. The first option is to take advantage of the fact that both the Netscape and Microsoft Web browsers can directly access a file system on a local computer without using a server (including a CD-ROM mounted on the computer's file system). These applications are commonly called "disk webs," and are used by book publishers to distribute CD-ROM versions of their publications. This approach is, in general, limited to static presentations such as book replicas. A disk web can limit its internal URL references to a restricted syntax called "relative addressing" in which the server is implied as the "current server" and is not actually specified in the URL. In this case, the same IETM system can be mounted on a JIA-compliant server or on a local computer's file system.

b. The second option is a legacy-data implementation and format for which an additional JIA-conforming Web-enabled presentation component has been developed that requires no alterations of the original electronic information for presentation on an intranet. In such a case, the same information can still be viewed on the original stand-alone viewer or on a JIA browser. External referencing may not work in this mode. If used, custom browsers should identify themselves.

5.   BROWSER COMPONENTS

5.1   Overview. The Web browser is an integral component of the Joint IETM Architecture that resides on the client side of the architecture. It should support the features needed by the server side that provide the functionality to the IETM. Because IETMs in the JIA may provide a range of capabilities to the user, the browser should be capable of supporting a range of features as well. Currently, there are two major browsers featuring competing technologies that may support IETM capabilities. Microsoft's Internet Explorer and Netscape's Navigator both support basic Web surfing capabilities. However, when higher level scripting is introduced, there is the chance that incompatibilities may be encountered. It is important to design the IETM to detect the type of browser in use by the client and provide the appropriate code to support that particular browser. The remainder of this section explains the minimum acceptable features of an intranet/stand-alone Web browser suitable for viewing technical manual data within the Department of Defense (DoD). Due to the expense and time involved in developing custom browsers, commercial browsers currently available on the market should be utilized. External referencing may not work in this mode.

5.2   Classification. The Web browser should conform to the following DoD parameters:

    a. Platform. The Web browser should be operable on the DoD Defense Information Infrastructure (DII) platforms approved by Defense Information Standardization Agency (DISA).

    b. Environment. The Web browser should be operable on a DoD Common Operating Environment (COE) approved by DISA, as well as the operating environment of the various infrastructures planned by the services in support of the DoD Global Combat Support System (GCSS).

    c. Architecture Applicability. This technical description affects the end user portion of the JIA as indicated in Figure 2.

The Architecture

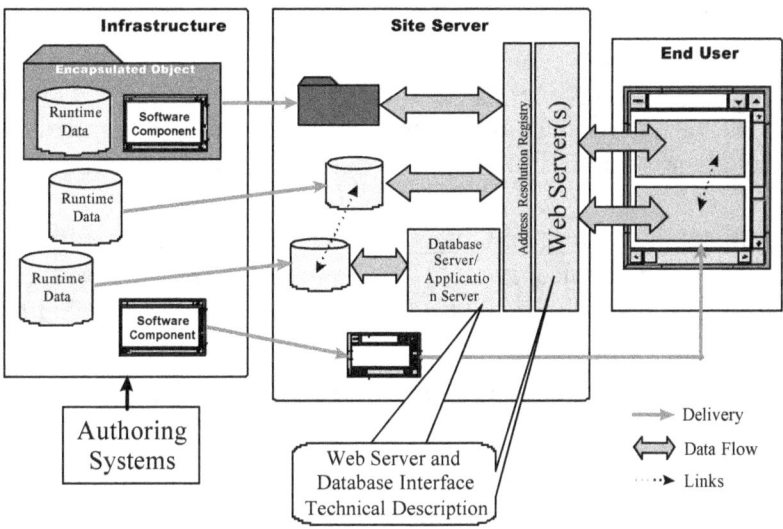

FIGURE 2. IETM Architecture Building Block

5.3   Salient characteristics. The World Wide Web (WWW) browser should support the following minimum features:

   a. Thin client/server model.

   b. Commercially defined object model.

   c. Browser should identify itself to the server.

   d. Commonly used internet transport and addressing protocols.

   e. Frames.

   f. DoD standardized controls, applets, or software components.

   g. User interface.

   h. Offline browsing.

   i. Hypertext markup language (HTML).

   j. Security.

k. Java.

l. Supported data types.

m. Multimedia.

5.3.1   <u>Thin Client/Server Model</u>. The browser should be a thin client, which necessitates Transmission Control Protocol (TCP)/Internet Protocol (IP) connectivity. This model assures that IETM data need not be permanently stored on the client machine.

5.3.2   <u>Commercially Defined Object Model</u>. The browser should support at least one commercially defined object model [i.e., Component Object Model (COM)/ Distributed COM (DCOM), Common Object Request Broker Architecture (CORBA)].

5.3.3   <u>Commonly Used Internet Transport and Addressing Protocols</u>.

a. File Transfer Protocol (FTP).

b. HyperText Transport Protocol (HTTP) 1.0/1.1.

c. Uniform Resource Locator (URL).

5.3.4   <u>Frames</u>. The browser should support the display of multiple frames, so that multiple presentations of information may be displayed simultaneously on a single screen.

5.3.5   <u>Extensible Components</u>. The browser should support extensible controls and add-on components to process data types not natively supported.

5.3.6   <u>User Interface</u>. The browser should support the following user interface capabilities:

a. Context Menus should be available to permit the user to utilize all features and options of the browser.

b. Tool tips should be made available to the user.

c. Configurable toolbars.

5.3.7   <u>Offline Browsing</u>. The browser should provide the ability to browse information on the client system without a permanent connection to a network.

5.3.8 HTML Support.

    a. HTML 3.2/4.0 Strict (with support for Cascading Style Sheets).

    b. Dynamic HTML should be made available using JavaScript as a minimum.

    c. Full-screen mode.

    d. Layers should be made possible using style sheets.

5.3.9 Security. The Web browser should provide security support for certificates, encrypted e-mail, and digital signatures, in accordance with the official DoD Public Key Infrastructure (PKI) policy.

    a. Personal Certificates. The Web browser should protect against fraud by providing support for certificates.

    b. Encryption. The Web browser should support FIPS 140 data encryption to protect the data during transmission.

    c. Digital Signatures. The Web browser should support the authentication of senders by supporting digital signatures.

5.3.10 Java.

    a. Java Virtual Machine. The Web browser should support a Java Virtual Machine.

    b. Just In Time (JIT) compiler. The Web browser may optionally support a JIT compiler to improve the speed of execution for Java applets.

5.3.11 Supported Data Types. The Web browser should support the following simple data types, either natively or with the use of add-on components:

    a. Hypertext Markup Language (HTML).

    b. Standard Generalized Markup Language (SGML).

    c. eXtensible Markup Language (XML).

    d. Portable Document Format (PDF).

    e. Computer Graphics Metafile (CGM).

    f. Joint Photographic Experts Group (JPEG).

    g. Tagged Image File Format (TIFF).

5.3.12 <u>Multimedia</u>. Components and plug-ins needed to support multimedia (e.g., video, animation, sound) should be provided by the IETM and not assumed to be supplied by the browser.

5.4   <u>Implementing Advanced Features</u>.

5.4.1   <u>eXtensible Markup Language (XML)</u>. It is believed that in the very near future XML will play a vital role in any Internet-based architecture. As of this date, Microsoft Internet Explorer 5.0 implements XML 1.0 and supports the transformation portion of eXtensible Style Language (XSL), albeit in a non-standard way. Netscape has announced that it, too, plans to offer XML support in the next version of Netscape Navigator (5.0) and will add XSL only when the standard is finalized.

5.4.2   <u>Java</u>. Both Netscape and Microsoft browsers contain Java Virtual machines, with Microsoft implementing a non-standard version containing Windows specific features. It is not known when or if Microsoft plans to modify its virtual machine to comply with Sun Microsystems' Java standard. Developers should either avoid the non-standard features, or alternatively use a free add-on product available for both browsers that replaces the built-in virtual machines with one developed by Sun. If this is done, an additional HTML tag should be added to the HTML page to launch the replacement Java virtual machine.

5.5   <u>Regulatory Guidance</u>. The security modules utilized by the browser should be validated for FIPS 140-1 conformance by the National Institute of Standards and Technology (NIST) in accordance with The Computer Security Act of 1987 and delegated by National Bureau of Standards.

6.   OBJECT ENCAPSULATION GUIDANCE

This section describes the guidance for the packaging and delivery of the IETM components. A fundamental principle underlying the Joint IETM Architecture is that developers of IETMs can deliver, as a single view package, all capability in the form of technical information and software components needed to install and use an IETM on a standard DoD intranet. This provides the IETM suppliers with a description of the framework in which they are to package and deliver the digitally encoded IETM. This view package contain both content and software components that have been combined into encapsulated objects and delivered as a contract package for electronic archiving or subsequent store-and-forward management. Consequently, there is no need for separate delivery of an IETM presentation device or piece of viewer software for separate installation onto the user's presentation device. Rather, the view package intrinsically contains the capability to be automatically installable onto the end-user intranet at the time it arrives at the intranet. The specific methodology for accomplishing this is not specified in this guidance.

6.1   Core Object Encapsulation. All components, content, and software should be encapsulated into a single IETM view package for transport to the user intranet in a form which is accessible and viewable on an end-user presentation device. It applies irrespective of the method employed for information delivery, whether on-line or via a high-density data bundle such as a CD-ROM.

The encapsulated (data and software) objects should eventually be delivered by the service infrastructure to the field-user activities as though they were simple binary data packages. These packages should be treated by the infrastructure as file-oriented data destined for a DoD site intranet Web-server. The view packages should appear simply as a generic "bucket of sequenced bits" that are processible by the server, but for which the content is of no concern to the infrastructure. The infrastructure activity need only assure that these bits remain packaged together. The view package is a set of industry-standard binary files, each of which is assigned a JIA notional locator (e.g., a URL, or Uniform Resource Locator, conforming to the JIA Electronic Addressing model) that contains sufficient information to support its installation as data in the intranet server file system. (See section 7 for details.) Until the point of receipt by the intranet server, the view package is processed as a single object. Only at the server is the view package broken down into its constituent parts.

The complexity and degree of integration of these view packages will vary greatly among differing IETMs. Some are simply a two-part collection of one software component and one data set. The simplest form should be a single set of data with all of the needed software contained in the standard JIA browser. In other forms, a system of software components and possible multiple data sets spreads out among several servers and the browser device when the IETM is operational. For example, this latter case might apply when there are background software agents that might be concurrently performing diagnostics and system monitoring. Another emerging technology needing the use of more complex IETM encapsulated objects entails the use of software agents acting as intelligent mentors which insert training aids into the job-aiding presentation when the agent (a computer program) determines they are needed. Between these extremes is a spectrum of complexity, each level recommending a somewhat different object-encapsulation approach. The "object" nature of such view packages is that all the intelligence needed to construct the operational IETM on the target intranet is contained within each view package object itself. Thus, there is no single standard for the internal constructs of the view package in the JIA, and the absence of such a standard is a distinct characteristic of the object-oriented approach used by the JIA.

6.2   Object Encapsulation for Various JIA Architecture Types. In practice, the implementation of an IETM intranet may be simple (as is the case with basic HTML pages) or more complex (as is the case with most custom servers) than that implied by the baseline operational flow of encapsulated objects (see Figure 1, section 4). The following breakdown of anticipated IETM view packages by architecture type is presented in order to categorize these variants and to provide guidance that is more specific in the implementation of these variants. These variants have been developed to reflect the reality of the differing approaches currently taken to implement large Web sites in the commercial sector. They are not intended to be a new specification of how IETMs should be developed differently. Any particular IETM intranet implementation typically contains a mixture of these types. The four architecture type categories described represent a continuous spectrum of variation rather than a discontinuous set. Thus, for some applications, it is difficult at times to categorize all implementations precisely. However, the overall guidance applies in all cases.

Definitions of these architecture types are given in Table II. The type definitions are grouped into two categories:

a. <u>IETM architecture types C1 and C2</u>. With type C object encapsulation, the various components of the IETM come together in the browser (i.e., client) software. The server merely manages the separate components for file and delivery purposes. No actual computations are performed on the site server. These types need only a browser and a generic HTTP based Web-server.

b. <u>Architecture types S1 and S2</u>. For type S object encapsulation, the computational process is hosted on the site server where the IETM software comes together with the IETM technical information and the server is the location where the computational processes are accomplished. Only the last step, that of rendering an image on the screen, is performed by the browser. For these server-centric types, the technology for incorporating the additional servers into a Web-type environment is less mature with respect to standardization, and available commercial products are much more diverse. This segment of the market place is just now emerging, and it is much dominated by proprietary products. However, the products have been developed to meet real commercial requirements and are very powerful for highly interactive presentations. They are in particular, effective for large-scale IETMs that are frequently updated from an authoring database.

TABLE II. IETM Architecture Types

Type	Characteristics	Examples
Type C1: **Basic HTML/ XML Pages**	HTML/ XML page(s) with only browser-resident components. Needs no component licensing. Most will work on any browser. Includes HTML 4.0 scripts. Client processing only. "Plain vanilla" HTTP server.	HTML with Java script, GIF, JPEG, frames XML + CSS or XSL Style Sheets When standardized by JIA Policy, PDF and CGM files.
Type C2: **Simple Down-loadable Component**	Viewer-specific data set plus custom automatically downloadable non-HTML viewing component Uses "plain vanilla" HTTP server.	.doc files plus MS WordView control Legacy Systems reprogrammed as custom browser or presentation system operating inside a standard browser shell/container.
Type S1: **HTML Plus Application Server**	Two-tier architecture in which Web page includes reference to server application(s), which must operate before page is delivered to client as HTML/ XML. Data and components managed on server. Utilizes File Base on Server. Needs HTTP server with S/W components for server-side computations. Permits both client *and* server processing.	MS Front Page Webs MS Design-time Controls CGI Server Apps DynaWeb
Type S2: **HTML with Database Server**	Three-tier architecture that includes a Web page server with pages functioning like a template; e.g., for calls to a database manager, which contains most of the IETM content. Can include server and components for custom functions. Needs a DBMS server (e.g., Oracle) in addition to the HTTP server. Permits both Client *and* Server processing.	Raytheon AIMSS 4.0 Boeing Data Courier GD TechSight Web MS ASP w/ODBC Calls

6.2.1   <u>Properties of Client-Based Architecture Types</u>. Architecture types C1 and C2 share the common important properties of not requiring installation or operation of unique software on the server. Thus, the server can be treated as an electronic bookshelf. As far as the server is concerned, the two parts of a type C2 encapsulated object (the content and the associated software components) are simply treated as files. Type C1 encapsulated objects have no included software components that need to be downloaded from the server. Additionally, any contemporary HTTP server can be employed and it does not matter what operating system is employed. Thus, for type C1 and C2 IETM applications, interoperability is very low-risk in the sense that, with these, any IETM view package can be accessed using any server. For IETMs of types C1 and C2, only a generic server is needed, without need for any JIA-specific server. Both types are considered pure encapsulated-object types; however, for type C1, the component part of the object can be implied (i.e., omitted), as its presence can be treated as preinstalled on any JIA-compliant browser and need not be included in the transported IETM view package. For type C2 encapsulation, the software component is downloaded from the server to the browser the first time the IETM is accessed.

The type C definitions are closely tied to specific versions of HTML and XML, a situation that is further clarified in this document. HTML/XML is herein specified as employing both HTML version 4.0 and XML version 1.0, both International W3C (World Wide Web Consortium) recommendations (i.e., de facto standards) which have been formally approved. An important consideration behind this decision is that essentially all the major software vendors support these W3C recommendations, whereas no complete agreement exists as to support of delivered products based on the previous HTML 3.2. The XML standard has elicited widespread vendor promise of support as a user-extensible expansion of HTML. XML lags behind HTML 4.0 in maturity, but the W3C recommendation is sufficiently complete so that software has been provided by major vendors and shows promise of becoming a Web-based tagging standard that is more suited to the preparation of complex IETMs than HTML. In particular, it should be much easier to convert the large DoD inventory of SGML-tagged source data to XML for a JIA-compliant presentation than it is to convert it to HTML.

Figure 3 illustrates a client-based architecture (types C1 and C2) with two kinds of software elements: Web browsers and Web servers. In general these are hosted on separate devices connected by a TCP/IP network [i.e., Local Area Network (LAN)]; however, an intranet can also be set up in a single display device without a network. In the case of IETM architecture types C1 and C2, these two kinds of elements are all that is needed.

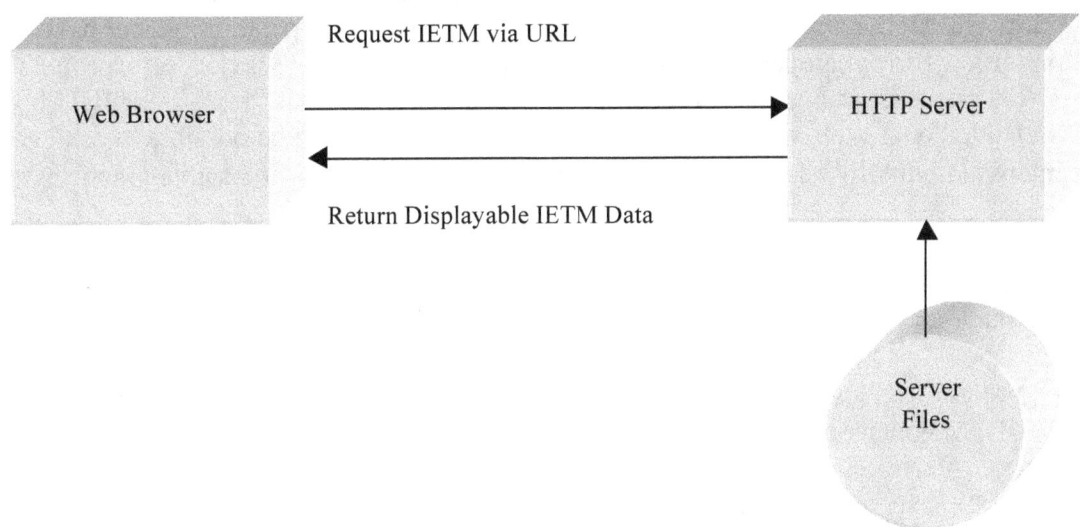

FIGURE 3. <u>Elements for Architecture Types C1 and C2</u>

6.2.2   <u>Properties of Server-Based Architecture Types</u>. For type S1 and S2 IETM applications, particularly for the server application software, current de facto industry practices for encapsulating the differing application server packages are much less certain to achieve the stage of W3C Recommendation. Several company-proprietary approaches are available for standardizing, such as Microsoft's design-time controls and Active Server Pages (ASP). Additionally, a variety of third-party middle-ware products exist to perform the integration of Web-servers and application servers. However, the technology and the state of de-facto industry standards are not sufficiently mature at this time to propose any one of them as a DoD standard, a practical necessity if all IETMs are to operate on a single server. However, this is not the only method to achieve operational interoperability with server-based solutions on a particular intranet. There are two possible approaches for a working solution:

a. The first is that the various IETM providers should put their own physical server(s) plus the IETM view packages on the user intranet (very feasible with the state-of-the-art and capacity of today's portable computers and plug-in network standards); or

b. The second is that all IETM creators should use the same set of server components (i.e., the application server) and install the standard components on all intranets employed in the community throughout which the IETMs are interoperable.

In general, the second approach is only feasible for a tightly controlled community and not applicable to the general DoD situation. With the current situation described above, multi-unit DoD forces, such as would be involved in a joint operation, would have to rely on option 1 for interoperability of application server based IETMs (i.e., S1 or S2). The JIA is intended, in this case, to be a facilitator to assure that this "bring your IETM preloaded on a Web-server" approach is feasible and it should be possible to achieve interoperability by adding the new server on the joint network, a feasible practice.

Figure 4 illustrates the architecture of type S1 for an additional element, the application server, sometimes referred to as a Web server extension because it effectively operates in the same operating system as, and is an extension of, the HTTP server.

Figure 5 illustrates the architecture of type S2 for a database server which hosts most of the IETM content and which may or may not be hosted in the same device as the intranet server. A type S2 application usually includes aspects of a type S1, since it needs an application server to process the information-access and request dialog between the intranet server and the separate database server. Note that while the distinction between these two types may, at times, not be clear, they differ in general as to where the primary information content is stored, i.e., in the server files or database management system (DBMS) managed databases.

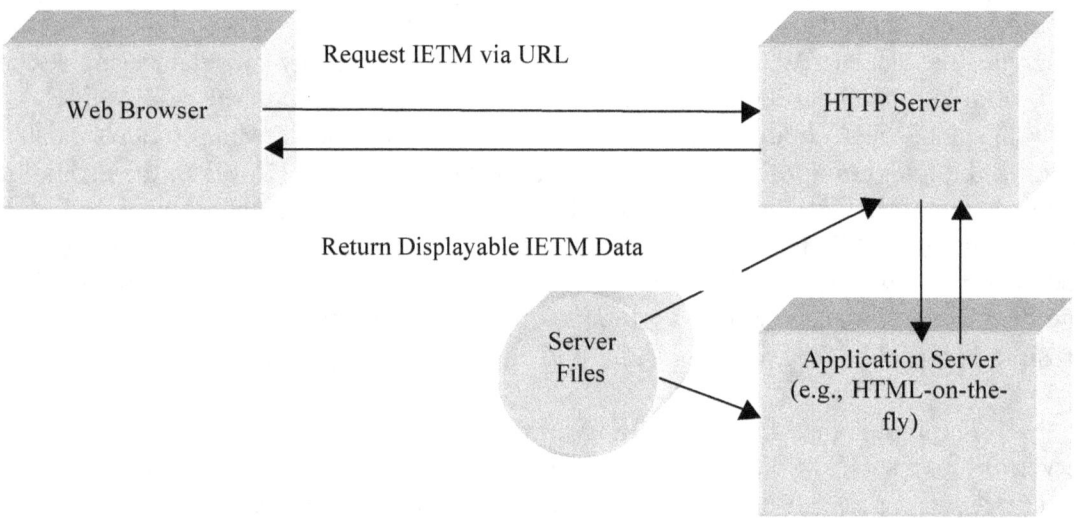

FIGURE 4. <u>Elements for Architecture Type S1</u>

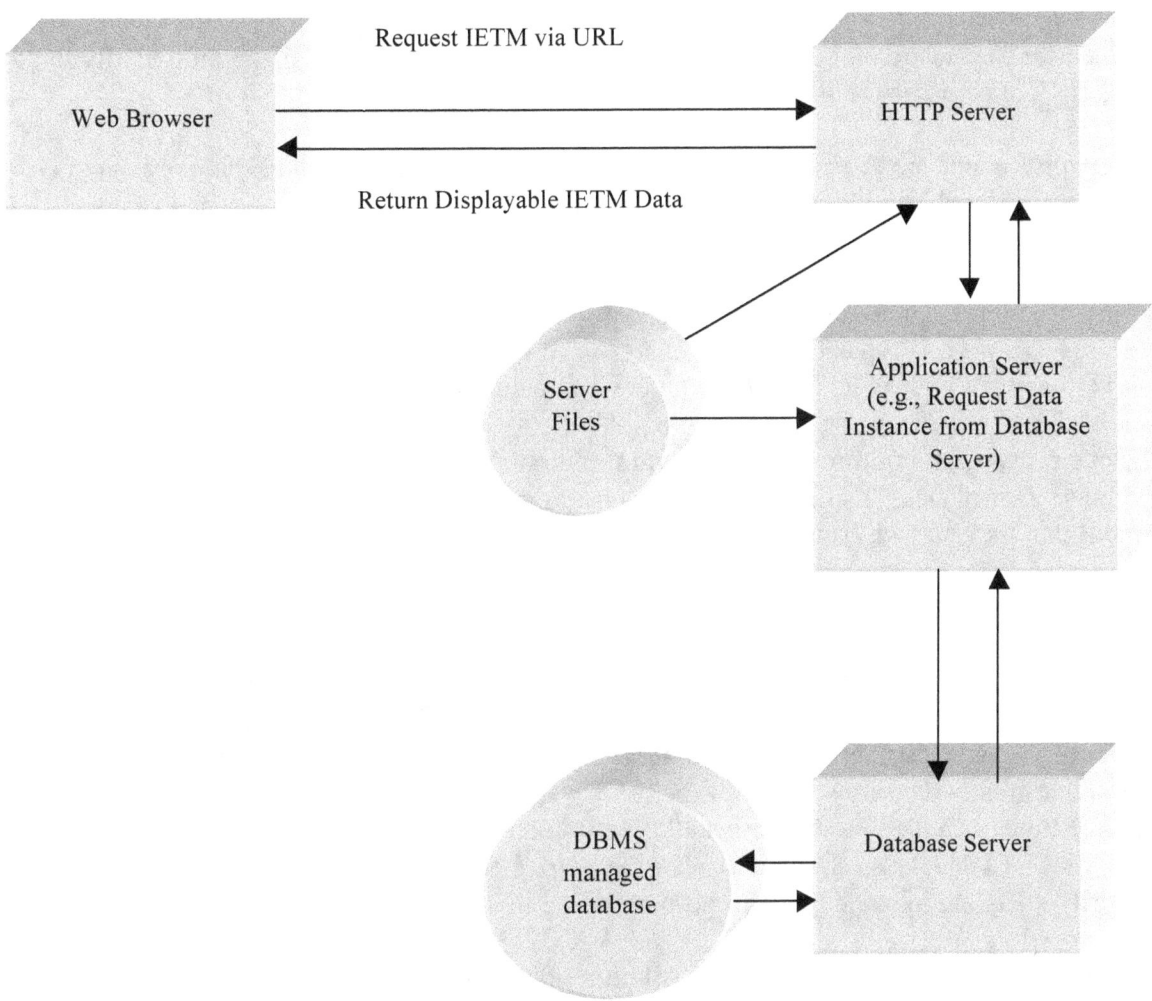

FIGURE 5. Elements for Architecture Type S2

6.2.3 <u>General Advisory for the Deployment of the Differing Architectural Types</u>. The following paragraphs are presented as optional guidance that can be followed if the IETM developer or program office customer believe they apply to their particular situation.

Where appropriate, the C1 type is much less problem prone and typically yields better performance that the other types, particularly when the IETM is principally preauthored and contains static information that remains the same from one presentation to the next. Since this is the case with most existing printed (legacy) technical manuals (TMs), a great deal of formerly printed TM material lends itself to Type C1 presentation. The format control needed to preserve the usability and contextual content of paper TMs is available with HTML 4.0 with Cascading

Style Sheets (CSS) and static XML-coded information. The technology is very good, and the preparation tools are inexpensive, but powerful, for most legacy-data conversion applications.

The high end of the spectrum, the type S2 application with a DBMS managing the information and including true interactive features such as context filtering and program sequences, is best suited to large weapon-system IETMs. An additional feature of all server-based systems is that it is much easier to manage the security features at the server rather that manage the security in every client that accesses the IETM server.

Type C2 applications are the most vulnerable to computer virus infection in that they may host computer viruses and bring them to the user device with a download. Every downloaded component should be very thoroughly screened upon downloading, often a daunting circumstance. As such, it is the advice of this document that the type C2 implementation should be limited to the presentation of legacy applications where it is cost-prohibitive to do other than this. In these cases it is typically less expensive to re-code the existing application as a plug-in than it is to convert over to a new authoring environment. Emerging DoD security concerns over downloadable components may render the employment of type C2 difficult to implement in a DoD system that must conform to the new information-assurance and operational-security restrictions. Downloadable software components are a major concern in such environments to the extent that they may be banned or severely restricted by cognizant external authority.

A possible compromise for the situation, in which a program manager deems it necessary to have a custom software component down-loaded to the client device, is to provide for a software-component install page which is separate from the IETM. This install page would meet the automatic-install recommendation for JIA-compliant downloadable components but would entail no actual IETM data display. This would permit the downloadable software component to be placed under greater security scrutiny at the time of download (e.g., virus scan, digital signature check, one time opening of software-install permission on the browser, etc.). Subsequent to that process, the IETM could be employed under the more efficient normal use mode (i.e., without all the security checking in place but with no permission to download software components).

The primary reason for electing a type S1 solution often comes as a result of the business case for a legacy conversion process. An application server-based Web front end to a legacy application is often the least expensive method of Web enabling a legacy application of any sort. However, at times the size of the type S1 file base may be a limitation in very large IETM data collections, in which case, the IETM would be better managed using an established database management environment intended for large data stores (i.e., type S2). JIA total object encapsulation (i.e., encapsulating the total unmodified legacy application with a Web front end) is primarily intended for use with existing legacy IETM systems. By creating a single interface to the legacy application and by packaging the application as described in this document, a legacy IETM may made to comply with the JIA standards.

In summary, it is advised that either type C1 or S2 implementations be used for new IETMs. C2 and S1 implementations should be limited to legacy conversions for which a substantial economic case can be made.

7. IETM ADDRESSING AND REGISTRY SOFTWARE

7.1   General. This section describes both an addressing model and registry for IETM components that are shared across two or more weapon systems or, in the future, two or more integrated logistic support domains.

7.1.1   Background. An addressing mechanism is needed to identify the location of IETM run-time object components. This is needed to assure that the locations of IETM components (referenced by hyperlinks in IETM electronic pages):

    a. follow specified naming conventions;

    b. assure that broken links to information are minimized; and

    c. support configuration management recommendations for the identification of and access to the correct versions of the IETM components.

7.1.2   Recommended Operational Capability. To provide interoperability of IETMs at the end-user level, IETM addresses need to:

    a. address external entities (resources), such as documents, procedures, illustrations, fault-isolation trees, Repair Parts & Special Tools Lists (RPSTLs), schematics, Illustrated Parts Breakdown (IPB) diagrams and work packages; and

    b. permit authors to identify IETM entities that may not be stored in the same local directory as the referencing entity.

If the IETM is networked, the addresses may point to external entities:

    a. on the same server, but in a different file or directory,

    b. on a different server in the same Internet domain, or

    c. on a different server in a different Internet domain.

If the IETM is stand-alone, the addresses may point to external entities:

    a. in a different file or directory or fixed media (hard disk drive), or

    b. in a different file or directory on the same or different removable media (e.g., CD-ROM).

7.1.3   Operational Environments. Operational environments for the addressing software include:

    a. Networked,

b. Detached, and

c. Stand-alone [using a Portable Electronic Display Device (PEDD)].

7.1.4 <u>Security Environment</u>. Addressing software should link to unclassified, sensitive information objects. If registry software is accessible via the Internet, security parameters should include:

a. Identification of clients and servers;

b. Authentication of clients, servers, and IETM entities; and

c. Data protection and confidentiality (see FIPS 140-1).

7.1.5 <u>Life Cycle Support</u> Addressing software implementations should minimize maintenance of addresses (changes in apparent locations of IETM entities to IETM components that reference them).

7.2 <u>Salient Characteristics of External Entity Addresses</u>. The specific implementation of the IETM addressing model is via the use of an external entity address which is embedded in one IETM for purpose of referencing and calling, upon user selection, another IETM.

7.2.1 <u>External Entity Address Description</u> The external entity address description describes the link-addressing block of the IETM Architecture. (See the End User block of Figure 6.)

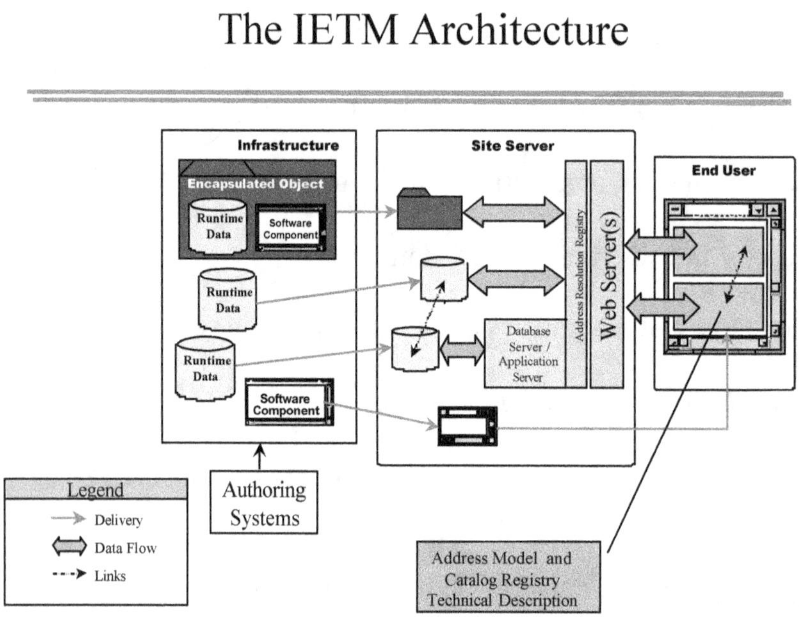

The IETM Architecture

FIGURE 6. IETM Architecture Building Blocks

7.2.2 <u>External Entity Address Features/Benefits</u>. A summary of external entity address features/benefits is shown below in Table III.

TABLE III. <u>IETM Entity Address Features and Benefits</u>

Feature	Benefit
Absolute Entity Addressing for HyperText Markup Language (HTML) 3.2 Documents	Supported by Commercial-Off-The-Shelf (COTS) Web servers and browsers; investment in legacy HTML IETM data is preserved.
Relative Entity Addressing for HTML 3.2 Documents	Supported by COTS Web servers and browsers; investment in legacy HTML and Portable Data Format (PDF) IETM data is preserved.
Parameter Passing to COTS Databases or Search Engines	Supported by COTS search engines, database, and other applications; web page content may be generated dynamically by Structured Query Language (SQL) parameter calls to a database; faster development, lower software maintenance cost for dynamically changing data.
Supports Standard Generalized Markup Language (SGML) and XML Public Entities	SGML legacy source data reuse leverages previous data acquisition costs.
Supports Addressing into Internal Structures of XML documents	Provides methods to address elements within a document such as an IPB diagram, specific maintenance or operational procedure.

7.2.3 <u>External Entity Address Specifications</u>. A summary of external entity address specifications is shown below in Table IV.

TABLE IV. <u>External Entity Address Specifications</u>

Attribute	Specification
Virtual Uniform Resource Locator (vURL)	Naming Convention for the location of shared IETM Components for a Weapon System
Uniform Resource Locator (URL).	Internet Engineering Task Force (IETF) Request For Comment (RFC) 1738
Relative URL	IETF RFC 1808
XML Public Entity	World Wide Web Consortium (W3C) XML 1.0 Recommendation (REC-XML-19980210)
XML Linking Language (XLink)	W3C XML Working Group: Working Draft 3/3/98
XML Pointer Language (XPointer)	W3C XML Working Group: Working Draft, WD-xptr-19980303

7.2.4   Minimum Criteria for External Addressing of Entities and Catalog Registry.

a. A virtual Uniform Resource Locator (vURL) should be identified, stored, and maintained for each location that represents a shared external entity (storage unit that is external to the current storage unit that is being displayed).

b. A minimum set of metadata (that is extensible to meet domain specific criteria) should be stored and maintained for each shared IETM object (or reusable component). A library model for the metadata and catalog registry should be maintained for the shared components.

c. A full-text search engine and index generator should be installed and maintained for both end-users and author/developers.

7.2.5   Virtual Uniform Resource Locator. The lead military service for a weapon system should establish and maintain a virtual Uniform Resource Locator (vURL) for each shared IETM entity. The vURL should represent a storage location for that shared external entity (storage unit that is external to the current storage unit that is being displayed). The attributes of the vURL structure (i.e., method://server/path/file [#anchor] [?query]) follow the naming structure of the World Wide Web Uniform Resource Locator as specified in Request for Comment (RFC) 1738. The vURL attributes are summarized in Table V.

TABLE V.   vURL Structure Attributes.

Attribute	Description
method:	Name of the HTML protocol method. "http" is the standard web protocol; others are: ftp, news.
Servername	Unique name of the host computer server address for the vURL (e.g., mil-service-activity.mil-service.mil) where mil-service-activity is the name of the military organization maintaining the vURL directory; mil-service is: (Navy, Army, AirForce, MarineCorps); and mil is the domain name following domain name conventions.
path/file	Directory path for IETM number; path naming convention may follow: /weapon-system/major-subsystem/sub-system/end-item tree hierarchy. Further break-downs may be needed to provide product/configuration management control.
[#anchor]	(optional) internal entity location identifier.
[? Query]	(optional) Database query statement to access a database in a three-tier IETM architecture configuration.

7.2.6 <u>Other vURL attributes</u>.

a. Persistent – actual physical address of the URL may change, but the vURL remains constant.

b. Actual Address – the current physical location of the entity – also follows the URL naming structure convention.

c. XML Linking Language (XLL) Attributes (work is still in process by the W3C XLL Working Group).

The vURL server should provide an alternate actual address in the event the server storing the primary physical address is not available (a "failover" capability).

7.3 <u>Initial Guidance for Establishing and Using vURLs</u>. The following guidance is offered for early developers of JIA-compliant IETMs. As discussed in this document, there are many factors to consider in developing a full and rich address model, however, it is critical that all DoD IETM developers adhere to some core model in the early stages of building the collection of interoperable JIA-compliant IETMs. Once published, a JIA compliant electronic address reference to a valid IETM external to the referencing IETM should never have to be changed in the referencing IETM, though the logical data may be updated. If deleted, the URL data request should return a "section canceled" (or some appropriate human readable message) by the referenced IETM. This type of permanent URL is called a persistent URL. In order to assure that URLs are indeed persistent URLs, the JIA recommends the use of virtual URLs (vURLs), as described below. These are URLs that use an administratively-assigned syntactically-correct server reference in the Internet URL syntax; however, the referenced server exists in name only. That is, a server by that name does not actually exist on the Internet or the DII and the name is used for data-management purposes only. When the IETM is actually installed on a intranet network, the vURL is remapped to the actual server on which the IETM data resides employing either the devices "Hosts" file and/or the IETM-specific Domain Name Services (DNS) in accordance with standard World Wide Web practices. The JIA-compliant intranet should establish the capability for the remapping of these vURLs, which reference a virtual server, into the actual server and file-system locations on the intranet under use. Initial guidance for establishment and use of vURLs is described in Table IV below.

Note

The criteria for JIA linking and addressing have not been established. Any implementation using JIA linking and addressing may need modification after the approved JIA linking and addressing is defined.

TABLE VI. Guidance for Establishing vURLs in the JIA

vURLs should be authored and maintained as follows:

HTTP should be the Web-page protocol to be utilized in this Architecture and construction of vURLs will use standard Internet conventions (i.e., the URL starts with "HTTP://" and is followed by ServerName/LibraryName/FileDirectoryBreakdown which may be terminated by a moniker [#, ?] followed by a parameter known to the target).

Format:
http://ServerName/LibraryName/FileDirectoryBreakdown[#or]MonikerParameter

ServerName is a unique name applying to the entire set of IETMs that is designed to operate from the same server. It will be assigned by the Service IETM registry. The specific rules for assigning such names will be determined by the Service IETM registries. [The assigned ServerName may be a single name (e.g., 'acb123server') or in the form of 'natsf.navy.mil' as though it were an actual server on the Intranet. If an Internet notation is employed, it is possible for a management activity to actually install such a server on the Intranet. They could maintain all of their cognizant URL references on that site in the form of acknowledgment as valid reference even if the actual content is not included on that site. However, the use of single names (i.e., no 'dots') is recommended to make it much clearer that a IETM-peculiar Domain lookup is needed when the IETM is mounted on an intranet. Single server names should be longer than 3 characters to eliminate the situation of being confused as an Internet domain such as 'mil' or 'org'.]

The LibraryName/FileDirectoryBreakdown breakdown notation should be unique across all DoD IETMs and should be administratively assigned as though it were the IETM number in the form of a Unix file-system reference with forward slashes such as "/navyietmlibrary/f18/ef/engine/ge/" or "/servicetmlibrary/tmnumber/systemnotation/…". The allocation of this "name space" will be managed by the Service IETM Registries. To permit distributed allocation authority, the higher (i.e., first) index field would be unique to the individual-Service registry. Additional Directory breakdown of files within the IETM reference is merely a further extension of the assigned FileDirectoryBreakdown name and content for a section within an IETM and may be null for the top-level reference.

 Sample: "/navyietmlibrary/f18/ef/engine/ge/diagnosis/test3".

Optional specific-IETM-defined monikers may be utilized. These are most commonly used for carrying a bookmark reference of a detailed database access parameters in the URL. These are indicated by a '#' or '?' at the end of the URL followed by a string of information which is processed by the IETM (and not the Web Server).

Thus, the JIA will need only that an Electronic-Addressing system exists and that it use the URL syntax. The administrative task of establishing, assigning, and enforcing the administration of the address space for IETMs should be the responsibility of some standing management activity that should manage an IETM Registry for each service.

7.4   IETM Object Metadata.   The IETM object metadata should be established and maintained to provide:

a. Object attributes used by search engines supporting a catalog registry – for entity/object sharing.

b. Configuration management of the object.

c. Life cycle maintenance of the object.

7.5   Metadata. The metadata should be extensible and at a minimum include:

a. Resource Description Framework (RDF) data including the Dublin Core Elements (work on the RDF is still in process by the W3C RDF Working Group).

b. Configuration Management Data including the TM number, revision date, and other information needed to identify specific configurations to which the object/entity is applicable.

c. Public Entity Names for SGML/XML document entities.

A library of objects together with the metadata should provide a "catalog" of IETM objects that may be reused from one weapon system configuration to another and from one ILSP domain to another. A database catalog should maintain this metadata. A registry process should be implemented to provide for the accession of new object metadata.

7.6   Search Engine.   A search engine should provide search services of the catalog registry and vURLs to provide access to authorized users to the metadata for each shareable object and the object's physical location. While this capability is intended primarily for authors/developers, it may also be provided to end-users to find supplementary technical information or updates to current information. The search engines should be implemented at infrastructure and end-user sites.

7.7   IETM Component Registry Description.

7.7.1   Background.   Current digital library models like the Navy's Advanced Technical Information Support (ATIS) system are CD-ROM based and need the user to provide a specific identification number to access the correct engineering drawing or technical manual. How is this information going to be indexed (e.g., IETM name, keywords, date, version) so that the correct information can be located rapidly and easily by the end user using a search engine? A related question is how the library should be organized so that different views or ways to access the library information may be available depending on the user's needs (e.g., How will IETM users locate and access IETM-related information like Equipment Identification Codes (EICs), Allowance Part Lists (APLs) and other information needed to perform maintenance, inspection, or operation of a weapon system or any of its components?). For example, on board a Navy ship, maintenance technicians are organized by work centers within divisions within departments. The end goal is to have this information accessible via a Web browser with the user's preferred view of the information.

7.7.2 <u>Recommneded Operational Capability</u>. To provide interoperability of IETMs at the end-user level, IETM components that will be referenced or accessed by external entities (other IETMs or their components):

 a. should be registered by each service;

 b. should provide a virtual address denoting the location of the entity;

 c. should provide other metadata to aid authors or end-users in the search and retrieval, and authentication of IETM components.

These external entities include resources such as documents, procedures, illustrations, fault-isolation trees, RPSTLs, schematics, IPB diagrams and work packages.

7.7.3 <u>Life Cycle Support</u>. Addressing software implementations should minimize maintenance of addresses (changes in apparent locations of IETM entities to IETM components that reference them). Additional life cycle support items for the registry include, for each IETM component:

 a. Weapon System Type Designator.

 b. End Item Designator [e.g., National Stock Number (NSN), Commercial And Government Entity (CAGE) Code].

 c. Technical Manual Identification Number.

 d. Technical Manual Type (maintenance, inspection, operations, other categories as defined by the services).

 e. Configuration Management Identifier.

 f. Security Classification Code.

 g. Distribution Code.

 h. Table of Related Reusable Components (e.g., figures, tables, audio clips, video clips).

 i. List of Related Joint Engineering Data Management Information and Control System (JEDMICS) Drawing Indexes and Drawing Numbers.

7.8 <u>IETM Object Registry Features/Benefits</u>. A summary of IETM object registry features/benefits is shown below in Table VII.

TABLE VII. IETM Component Registry Features/Benefits

Feature	Benefit
List of IETM components by end item	Data entity (illustration, maintenance procedure, illustrated parts breakdown, RPSTL) reuse by developers/authors for training and other Integrated Logistics Support Plan (ILSP) domains.
List of IETM components shared by two or more logistic ILSP domains	Shows where component is used across logistic domains; helps maintain distribution lists for planned updates/modifications Engineering Change Proposals (ECPs).
List of IETM components shared by two or more end items	Shows where component is used within a weapon system or across two or more weapon systems. Identifies IETM components needing update when an ECP or Pre-Planned Product Improvement (PPPI) is planned or implemented.

7.9   IETM Object Registry Specifications. A summary of IETM object registry specifications is shown below in Table VIII.

TABLE VIII. IETM Component Registry Specifications

Attribute	Specification
URL	IETF RFC 1738
Relative URL	IETF RFC 1808
XML Public Entity	W3C XML 1.0 Recommendation (REC-xml-19980210)
XML Link (XLink)	W3C XML Working Group: Working Draft 3/3/98
XML Pointer (XPointer)	W3C XML Working Group: Working Draft 3/3/98
XML Style Language (XSL)	W3C XML Working Group: Working Draft 3/3/98
XML Style Language Transform (XSLT)	W3C XML 1.0 Recommendation (REC-xml-19980210)
Resource Metadata	W3C Resource Description Framework (RDF)

7.10   URLs and File Pathname Locators for Legacy Applications. In general, a URL complete with a Server reference (or a relative reference relating to such a reference) should be used for addressing. Legacy applications which are dedicated to a particular device may utilize a URL (if in network connected mode) or legacy command line resource identifier (drive, directory path and file name, if in stand-alone mode or in network connected mode) to identify an IETM resource that is external to the calling IETM resource. However, it should clearly be noted that such a mechanism is not interoperable if the IETM is ever relocated from the dedicated device. As such, such an addressing mechanism should be avoided if at all possible.

7.11 Service Points of Contact for vURL Registration Based on current responsibilities, it is recommended by this the Tri-Service IETM Technology Working Group that the following organizations be responsible for the centralized registration of vURLs within their respective branch of Service:

    a. Army – LOGSA

    b. Navy – NAVAIR, NATEC

             – NAVSEA / SPAWAR, NSDSA

    c. Air Force – OC-ALC/TILUB

    d. Marine Corps – MARCORSYSCOM.

8.   WEB SERVER/CLIENT/STAND-ALONE IMPLEMENTATION GUIDANCE

8.1   Overview.

8.1.1   The Joint IETM Architecture. The Joint IETM Architecture (JIA) provides a framework for achieving interoperability among Interactive Electronic Technical Manuals (IETMs) using Web technology on Department of Defense (DoD) Intranets. The JIA enables interoperability at several levels. These levels include display of IETM data on a common browser; support of dissimilar (including proprietary) data structures and formats through the common browser interface; creation of composite IETMs from diverse, and possibly distributed, sources; and interchange and reuse of individual IETM components in multiple applications. This section supports the JIA by describing the implementation of Web servers and database servers that satisfy the interoperability goals. Figure 7 illustrates the features of the JIA and shows those parts of the architecture that are addressed within this document.

The Architecture

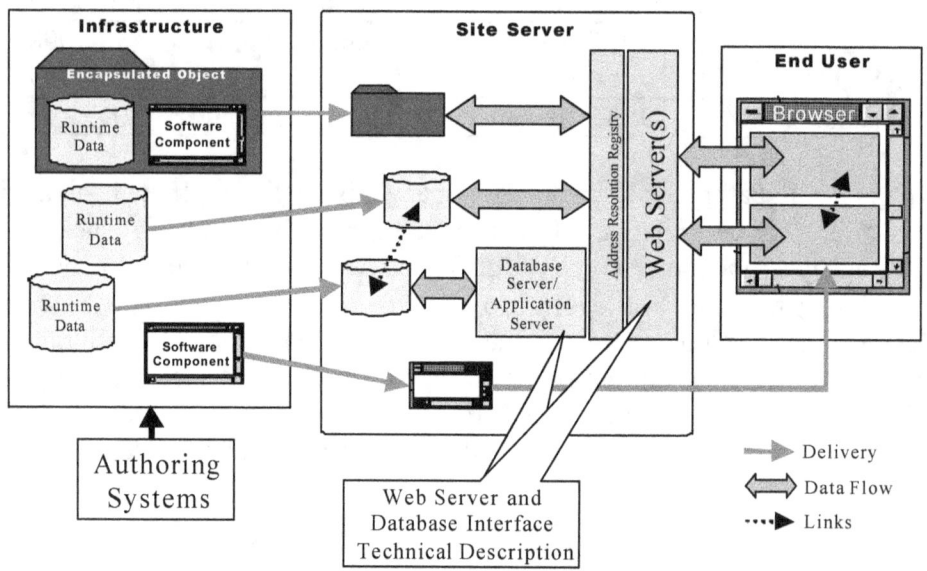

FIGURE 7. Illustration of the Key Parts of the JIA with Principal Web Server and Database Interface Components Identified

8.1.2 Connectivity of IETMs. Three cases are considered for connectivity of IETMs, including end-user platforms that are always, sometimes, or never connected to a network. IETM applications developed for these end-user platforms are described in terms of the following architectures:

a. Networked client/server applications.

b. Occasionally connected applications.

c. Stand-alone applications.

8.1.3 Off-the-Shelf Web Servers. The simplest way for the JIA to achieve IETM interoperability for the DoD IETM community is to use off-the-shelf Web servers with widely available server extensions. Such an approach requires no additional software to be overtly installed on either the servers or the browser device, although some supporting software components (e.g., applets, plug-ins, or controls) are likely to be automatically installed as the application is executing.

8.1.4 Legacy IETM Systems. Some legacy IETM systems, and possibly some highly innovative new IETM applications, may need additional, custom server extensions and database interface components. In these applications, there may be a strong business case for some agencies, programs, or companies to use or develop their own Web servers (e.g., Oracle Web Server) and custom server extensions, rather than relying on prepackaged solutions. Because of these cases, we should allow for the possibility of multiple simultaneously running Web and database servers on both stand-alone and occasionally connected networked configurations.

8.2 Networked Client/Server IETM Applications. In the networked client/server IETM application it is assumed that the end user device is connected to a network and communicates with one or more additional computers as shown in Figure 8. In this scenario, the end user device contains the necessary client application software and communicates with a Web server and/or database server.

Multiple Web and Database
Servers Supporting IETMs

Identically Configured
End User Devices

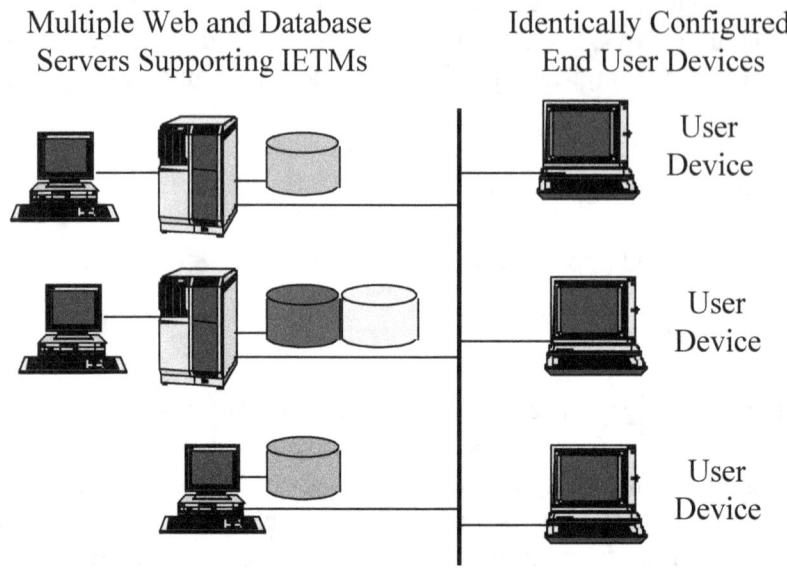

User
Device

User
Device

User
Device

FIGURE 8. Networked Client/Server IETM Applications

8.2.1   Web Server Support and Implementation.

8.2.1.1 The Networked Approach. The networked client/server IETM application places few
restrictions on the nature of the Web server. The networked client/server architecture enables
distributed applications where source data may exist on multiple platforms anywhere on a
network. Each server may be responsible for providing access to one or more IETM
applications. The advantage of the networked configuration is that a single user device with a
JIA browser can access multiple diverse and possibly distributed IETM data sources. This
approach provides the same advantages as an Internet-connected Web browser, except that the
data is provided in a more controlled Intranet environment. This networked approach is highly
recommended for IETM applications, where appropriate. The goal of the JIA is for Web servers
to provide the IETM data to software components that exist and execute on the client, hosted
within a JIA browser. Additionally, the networked client/server configuration enables the use of
customized server-based applications that usually function to dynamically convert specific data
formats and database data for JIA-compliant display. To fulfill the goals of the JIA, the key part
of compliant applications hinges on the linking and addressing mechanisms. The Web server
will be responsible for resolving addresses either directly (e.g., via a host table) or through an
interfacing application [e.g., a virtual Uniform Resource Locator (vURL) server].

8.2.1.2 Use of Customized Server Applications and/or Extensions. Use of customized server
applications and/or extensions [e.g., Common Gateway Interface (CGI) scripts, Internet
Information Server Application Programming Interface (ISAPI) applications, or FrontPage
extensions] limits the portability of IETM data among different Web servers and operating
systems. IETMs developed using Commercial-Off-The-Shelf (COTS) Web servers without
custom extensions generally have a higher degree of portability. If portability over server

platforms is desired an IETM should be constructed such that all execution logic that is needed is passed to the client.

8.2.1.3 Networked Client/Server Configuration Features. In the networked client/server configuration, the following features are the recommended minimum set for Web servers within the JIA:

a. Information Infrastructure (DII)/Common Operating Environment (COE) or other relevant policy directives.

b. Binding of multiple domain names to a single Internet Protocol (IP) address using host headers.

c. Supports HyperText Transport Protocol (HTTP) 1.1 or higher. Supports multiple ports.

d. Supports automatic Uniform Resource Locator (URL) redirection. Supports search engine.

e. Automatically re-indexes when a file is changed, added, or deleted. Supports File Transfer Protocol (FTP).

f. Password/challenge-response authentication. Digital certificate authentication.

g. Secure Socket Layer (SSL) 3.0. CGI and/or WinCGI.

h. Netscape Server Application Programming Interface (NSAPI) or ISAPI. Allows Server Side Includes (SSIs).

i. Supports server-side scripting languages [e.g., Active Server Page (ASP)] and/or Java servlets.

8.2.2 Database-driven IETM Applications. The networked client/server IETM application scenario is the ideal scenario for supporting and providing access to multiple and diverse database-driven IETMs. This networked configuration allows for the IETM data to be stored in multiple interconnected physical locations rather than on the end user device itself [on its hard drive or through Compact Disk - Read Only Memory (CD-ROMs) or Digital Video/Versatile Disk - Read Only Memory (DVD-ROMs)]. To support the goals of the JIA, these networked database-driven IETM applications should, at a minimum, be constructed such that the IETM data is presented within a JIA-compliant Web browser and utilizes the JIA linking and addressing mechanisms. The JIA linking and addressing mechanisms should be used for linking to internal and external data. The JIA linking and addressing scheme may also allow for linking from external IETM applications into the networked database-driven IETM applications. Such linking may need system-specific addressing schemes that are appended to the standard URL linking syntax. JIA linking and addressing mechanisms may be used for internal linking. By using the JIA addressing mechanism for internal linking, external links from the IETM are capable of going to the specific data object versus the "front page".

8.2.3 <u>Application Development Considerations</u>.

8.2.3.1 <u>Servers and Server-side Applications</u>. Servers and server-side applications that are capable of performing on the public World Wide Web (WWW) will also operate on DoD Intranets. However, server-side scripts and applications may need specific Web server products to operate properly. Such products could have licensing fees and agreements, particular hardware configurations, or specialized knowledge for proper installation and maintenance. Similarly, database servers may have special criteria and most likely be proprietary systems that have licensing agreements.

8.2.3.2 <u>Installation of Multiple Web Servers or Multiple Database Servers</u>. Installation of multiple Web servers or multiple database servers on a single hardware platform could be problematic. This operational consideration can more easily be overcome in a networked environment than in the occasionally connected and stand-alone cases described below by adding more hardware servers.

8.3 <u>Occasionally Connected IETM Applications</u>. The occasionally connected IETM application scenario, although complex, is ideal for supporting both networked and stand-alone IETM operation. This configuration enables the replication of part or all of an IETM database onto a portable end-user device, creating a mobile database. IETM applications that make modifications or additions to the mobile IETM database that are to be reflected back in the master database should include the appropriate synchronization and replication mechanisms to accomplish this. The occasionally connected IETM application scenario is illustrated in Figure 9.

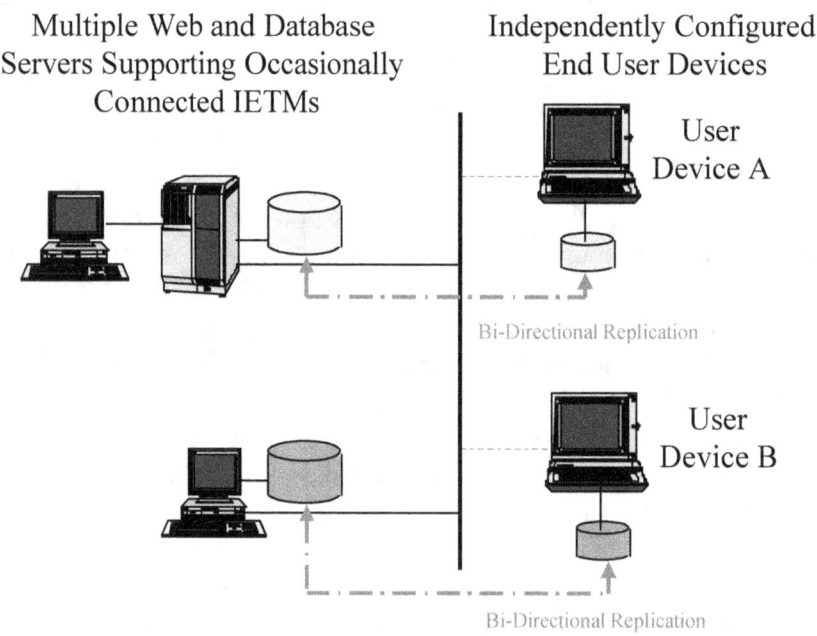

FIGURE 9. <u>Occasionally Connected IETM Applications</u>

8.3.1   <u>Web Server Support and Implementation</u>. The JIA recommends that software be designed to run on an Intranet, which implies that a Web server will be assumed to be available for delivering the IETM to users. Because the occasionally connected case needs software to run in both a connected and disconnected mode, the Web server should be capable of running on both a server platform and a client computer. The client-side Web Server may be accomplished using a Web server product designed specifically for that purpose. In addition, IETMs that access data from a variety of distributed server platforms could need more than one Web server installed. While this is possible, it obviously complicates the disconnected case. The case is simplified to the extent that Web server types can be limited to a minimum number.

8.3.2   <u>Addressing in the Occasionally Connected Mode</u>. According to the JIA, addressing of IETM components follows the Web convention URLs. (See section 7.) Because URLs are fixed pointers, they should be remapped when source information is moved. This is the case for occasionally connected systems, as source information moves from distributed locations to local drives just prior to disconnecting. The Addressing Model Technical Description provides guidelines for accomplishing the re-mapping of IETM sources and links when client systems are connected and disconnected.

8.3.3   <u>Occasionally Connected Mode Features</u>. In the occasionally connected configuration, the following features are the recommended minimum set for Web servers installed on either server or client hardware for use within the JIA.

a. Operation on the platforms and operating systems dictated by DII/COE or other relevant policy directives.

b. Binding of multiple domain names to a single IP address using host headers.

c. Supports HTTP 1.1 or higher.

d. Supports multiple ports.

e. Supports automatic URL redirection.

f. Built-in search engine.

g. Automatically re-indexes when a file is changed, added, or deleted. Supports FTP.

h. Password/challenge-response authentication.

i. Digital certificate authentication.

j. SSL 3.0.

k. CGI and/or WinCGI.

l. NSAPI or ISAPI.

m. Allows SSIs.

n. Supports server-side scripting languages (e.g., ASP) and/or Java servlets.

8.3.4 Database-driven IETM Applications in the Occasionally Connected Mode. As with networked applications, the JIA recommends that occasionally connected IETM applications should, at a minimum, be constructed such that the IETM data is presented within a JIA-compliant Web browser and implement the JIA linking and addressing mechanisms. The JIA linking and addressing mechanisms should be used for linking to both internal and external data. The JIA linking and addressing scheme should also allow for linking from external IETM applications into the occasionally connected database-driven IETM applications.

8.3.4.1 Linking and Addressing. In the occasionally connected configuration, the mechanisms for linking and addressing are complicated by the fact that the mobile subsets of the master database that are replicated on the end-user device may contain links to data that may not exist in the mobile database. In such occurrences, the user should be notified that the end user device should reconnect with the master database to obtain the data. Upon reconnection, ideally, the necessary data should then be transferred to the end-user device in a way that needs minimal effort on the part of the end user.

8.3.4.2 Multiple Database-driven IETMs. The occasionally connected configuration is also complicated by the fact that individual sites may utilize multiple database-driven IETMs. In such cases it may be difficult for individual end-user devices to support the processing and presentation of data from multiple dissimilar mobile databases. Such a case might occur, for example, if an IETM for an aircraft is developed using an Oracle database and the IETM for the aircraft's engine is developed using a Sybase database. In the networked configuration, this situation is easily handled by utilizing multiple computers with their own Web and database servers (one for each database). If designed properly, the networked end-user device with a Web browser could then access either or both databases without needing resource-intensive database software on the end-user device itself. In the occasionally connected configuration, however, the situation is much more complex because the portable end-user device would have to be capable of running all necessary Web server and database server software (in addition to the JIA Web browser).

8.3.5 Application Development Considerations.

8.3.5.1 Custom Server-side Applications, Extensions, or Databases. Client computers detached from the network should be capable of running Web servers, replicating databases, and hosting database servers that are needed by the IETM application. From a developer's perspective, it is important to anticipate various scenarios for an IETM application to access multiple, differing Web or database servers. It is recommended that occasionally connected IETM applications eliminate the need to use custom server-side applications, extensions, or databases to the extent practical.

8.3.5.2 <u>Automated Replication of Databases</u>. Where databases and database servers are implemented in the IETM, automated replication of databases is desirable. Partial replication of relevant parts of an IETM is important where the distributed database size exceeds the capacity of local storage, or where it is important to provide specific configurations of data for focused application. Support of partial replication should be provided as part of the IETM software package and may need customization for a meaningful user interface.

8.4   <u>Stand-alone IETM Applications</u>. The stand-alone database-driven IETM application scenario, shown in Figure 10, exists for those situations where neither networked nor occasionally connected configurations are desirable. In the stand-alone configuration, all IETM data is either on the hard-drive of the end-user device or is on one or more CD-ROMs, DVD-ROMs, or other portable storage devices.

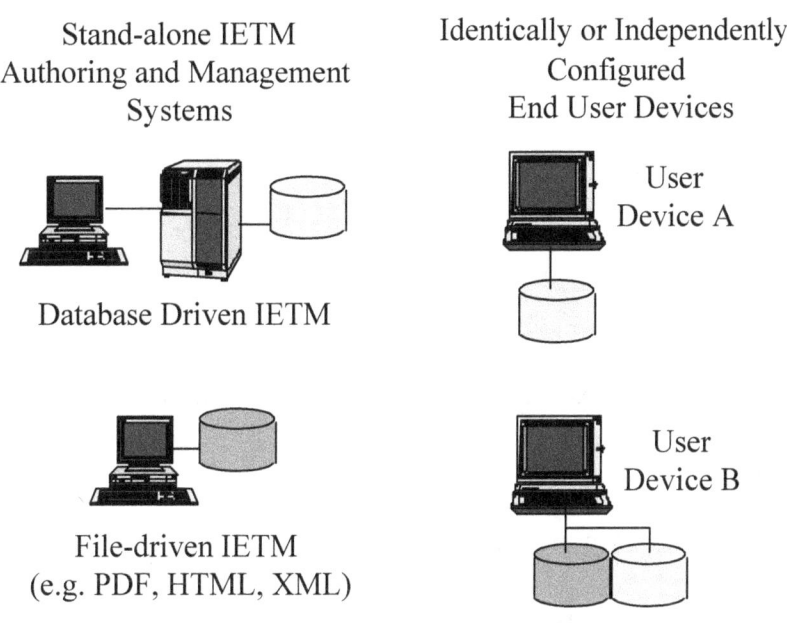

Stand-alone IETM
Authoring and Management
Systems

Identically or Independently
Configured
End User Devices

Database Driven IETM

User
Device A

File-driven IETM
(e.g. PDF, HTML, XML)

User
Device B

FIGURE 10. <u>Stand-alone IETM Applications</u>

8.4.1   <u>Web Server Support and Implementation</u>. To fulfill the goals of the JIA, the key parts of compliant applications hinge on the linking and addressing mechanisms and presentation of IETM data within a JIA browser. The need for a Web server on the stand-alone user device can be established on a case by case basis. Additionally, although the use of component software is recommended, it is not mandated.

8.4.1.1 <u>Web Servers and Stand-alone Configurations</u>. One of the issues associated with the stand-alone configuration is the use of Web servers. If multiple IETM applications are developed independently and are designed to use Web servers (although the end-user device is not connected to a network), then there may be cases where multiple simultaneously running Web servers must be installed. Each Web server would have to listen on a different port (although the port does not communicate with sources that are external to the end-user device).

These situations should be handled carefully and may result in software conflicts and would be resource intensive in terms of available memory and processor load. Although Web servers seem unnecessary in the stand-alone configuration, they may be desirable for many reasons. For example, applications designed with a Web server interface would enable future connectivity and interoperability with other applications on the stand-alone machine, or reuse of applications originally designed to operate in a JIA network or occasionally connected mode.

8.4.1.2 <u>Stand-alone Configuration Features</u>. In the stand-alone configuration, the following features are the recommended minimum set for Web servers within the JIA:

a. Operation on the platforms and operating systems dictated by DII/COE or other relevant policy directives.

b. Binding of multiple domain names to a single IP address using host headers.

c. Supports HTTP 1.1 or higher.

d. Supports multiple ports.

e. Supports automatic URL redirection.

f. Supports search engine.

g. Automatically re-indexes when a file is changed, added, or deleted.

h. Supports FTP.

i. Password/challenge-response authentication.

j. Digital certificate authentication.

k. SSL 3.0.

l. CGI and/or WinCGI.

m. NSAPI or ISAPI.

n. Allows SSIs.

o. Supports server-side scripting languages (e.g., ASP) and/or Java servlets.

8.4.2 <u>Database-driven IETM Applications in the Stand-alone Mode</u>. As with networked and occasionally connected applications, the JIA recommends that stand-alone IETM applications should, at a minimum, be constructed such that the IETM data is presented within a JIA-compliant Web browser and implement the JIA linking and addressing mechanisms. The JIA linking and addressing mechanisms should be used for linking to both internal and external data.

Note that external data refers to data that exists outside of an individual IETM (or IETM view package, work package, IETM database, or IETM data instance). In the stand-alone configuration, the external data may actually be on the same or separate internal hard-drive or may be on the same or separate CD-ROM or DVD-ROM. The JIA linking and addressing scheme should also allow for linking from external IETM applications into the stand-alone database-driven IETM applications.

8.4.3 <u>Application Development Considerations</u>.

8.4.3.1 <u>Linking and Addressing</u>. In the stand-alone configuration, the linking and addressing mechanisms are complicated by the fact that external links to IETMs may need access to multiple CD-ROMs or other storage devices. In these cases, the user should be notified as to which CD-ROM (or other device) should be inserted to access the data. The application should be designed in a way that needs minimal effort on the part of the end user.

8.4.3.2 <u>Multiple Database-driven IETMs</u>. The stand-alone configuration is also complicated by the fact that individual sites may utilize multiple database-driven IETMs. In such cases it may be difficult for individual end-user devices to support the processing and presentation of data from multiple dissimilar database-driven IETMs. The considerations here are similar to those for the occasionally connected configuration. The portable end-user device should be capable of running all necessary Web server and database server software (in addition to the JIA Web browser).

9. MAINTAINING A COMMON LOOK-AND-FEEL AMONG DIFFERING IETMs

While the use of the common browser does standardize many of the user-interaction features, it is very likely that a custom component will contains its own set of unique user-interaction features layered under the higher-level browser toolbars. These features often conform to a proprietary look-and-feel dictated by the COTS product being employed. However, the need for a procurement-guidance document which can be employed to minimizing the differences in look-and-feel among various disparate IETM presentation components that operate in the JIA environment still exists. From both the Training and the Job Performance perspective, the effectiveness of each product is enhanced when it is displayed in accordance with a standard style, even if the actual underlying IETM presentation components vary and are proprietary in nature.

9.1 <u>Joint DoD/Industry User-Interaction Guidelines</u>. A preliminary set of standard "look-and-feel" recommendations is included in this handbook. It may be used to prepare guidance for the suppliers of IETMs and IETM software products. These guidelines permit the use of contractor selected authoring and presentation products while, at the same time, preserving the essence of a common DoD look-and-feel if the software products adhere to the guidelines. These guidelines are the result of a workshop between members of the individual Services (selected by the Tri-Service IETM Technology Working Group members) and the Aerospace Industries Association (AIA) Service Publications Panel. The guidance contained herein greatly reduces the existing performance requirements to those few that are really needed, and tightens down those few remaining recommendations to be as specific as possible. The intent is that these guidelines eventually replace the user-interaction requirements sections of MIL-PRF-87268, *Manuals, Interactive Electronic Technical: General Content, Style, Format, and User-Interaction.*

IETM TMCRs (Technical Manual Contract Requirements) and other procurement instruments may specify that delivered IETM view packages conform to both the JIA performance recommendations and the included look-and-feel user-interface recommendations. By doing so, it will be possible to obtain a meaningful level of common DoD IETM look-and-feel interface without needing the acquisition of a custom IETM system.

9.2   Preliminary User-Interaction Guidelines for DoD IETMs. The following is a preliminary set of IETM User-Interaction ("look-and-feel") guidelines and should be observed in preparing IETMs and the associated viewing software components for the Department of Defense:

9.2.1   Display Format (text/font, graphic, table, lists, object embedding).

   a. Use best commercial practices.

   b. Use of multiple frames is not a requirement.

9.2.2   Browse Capability. Browse capability should be available.

   a. User controlled access mode.

   b. No tracking of activities.

   c. Not rigidly tied to IETM controls.

9.2.3   Link Behavior/Navigation.

   a. Persistent visual indication of link(s) to additional information should be available.

   b. There should be a visual indication of how the link behaves (e.g., goto, gosub, relational).

   c. If you are executing a link that is not a goto or exit link, you should be able to return to the link source from the link destination.

9.2.4   Control Bars.

   a. The User Navigation Panel (Tool Bar) should provide the necessary choices/options available at the current time.

   b. The User Navigation Panel is needed with an optional toggle capability to turn it off.

   c. The User Navigation Panel should remain accessible by persistent visible indication.

d. Use the standard icons when applicable in the User Navigation Panel.

9.2.5   Icon Standardization

a. An icon should show its name or function when the cursor is stalled over the icon.

b. Suggested Icons for standardization:

1. Next
2. Previous [Chronological]
3. Return [Chronological]
4. Back [Logical]
5. TOC
6. Exit
7. Find/Search
8. Undo
9. User Navigation Panel Minimized
10. Processing Indication
11. Parts (IPB/RPSTL)
12. Suggested Changes/Feedback
13. Training
14. Multimedia Icon
15. Sound/Voice Icon
16. Full Motion Video Icon
17. Animation Icon
18. Graphic
19. Diagnostics
20. Wiring Diagrams
21. Acronyms
22. Abbreviations
23. Help
24. Version Info.
25. Warning
26. Caution

27. Note

28. Hazards Icons such as those included in MIL-STD-38784

29. Print

30. One way link (Goto)

31. Two way link (Gosub)

32. Relational link

33. Browse

9.2.6   Selectable Elements (Hot-Spots).

a. All Hot Spots should be visually indicated (e.g., fill pattern, reverse video, outline, button, underline).

b. There should be an indication of link destination (target) when the cursor passes over the hot-spot.

c. There are three acceptable modes of visual indication of hot-spots (selectable areas).

1. Persistent visual indication that an area is hot.

2. Cursor changing shape/color.

3. Object changes while cursor over area (e.g., IPB callout expands).

9.2.7   Warnings, Cautions, Notes.

a. User should acknowledge pop up warnings and cautions before proceeding.

b. Pop up alerts should be centered on the screen.

c. A persistent icon should appear on the screen when alert is applicable.

d. Standard colors for alerts: Red – Warning, Yellow – Caution, Cyan – Note.

9.2.8   Search & Lookup.

a. Use the standard icon to get the user into a search mode.

b. The user should be presented with the search options available.

c. At a minimum, a Keyword search against valid entry points (TOC/List of Content) should be available.

d. The system should provide a search capability against Metadata (e.g., Keywords, tagged data, indexable data, searchable data, etc.) when it exists.

9.2.9 Session Control (Suspend, Resume, Nested Sessions).

a. The user should be able to suspend a session at any time (e.g., for a break or emergency).

b. A resume function should be capable of re-starting the session at the same point it was suspended.

c. At the time of resume, the user should be advised that some key parameters/condition settings may be out-of-date (e.g., aircraft safe for maintenance, temperature change, or other people worked on the end-item/platform during the suspension).

d. The system should support the three Exit Modes:
   1. Complete   (Save and update history)
   2. Abort   (Don't save or update history)
   3. Suspend   (See a. above).

9.2.10 Context Filtering.

a. The system should have the ability to perform context filtering on effectivity as a minimum.

b. The system should provide the user a mechanism for entering/modifying configuration parameters.

9.2.11 Screen Resolution and Color Guidelines.

a. Presentation system and graphics developers should consider the use of standard "safe" colors visible across multiple presentation systems.

b. Presentation systems should not presume any fixed display resolution, or size.

9.2.12 Information Access (Indices, Electronic TOCs, etc.).

a. A Table/List of all key entry points should be made available for user access.

b. Access should be provided via a Hierarchical Breakdown such as:

   1. SSSN (MIL-STD-1808)
   2. LCN
   3. AECMA 1000D
   4. Functional and Physical Hierarchy

c. Graphical Interfaces are acceptable.

9.2.13 <u>Dialogs</u>.

a. Support should be provided for both pop-up dialog box and in-line dialogs in the display frame itself.

b. Developers should use best commercial practices for entering data in dialog boxes (e.g., radio buttons, check-boxes, fill-ins, combo boxes, scrolling selection lists, etc.).

9.2.14 <u>Sound</u>.

a. Developers should use best commercial practices when implementing sound.

b. The user should take action to hear the sound. (No automatic playing of sound.)

c. User controls muting and volume via system controls (versus embedded controls within the application). Optional: Application can provide convenient access to the system controls.

9.2.15 <u>Voice Input/Output (I/O)</u>.

a. Voice I/O should be used only as supplemental input/output and navigation.

b. Keyboard and pointing devices should be the primary input, and visual display should be the primary output.

9.2.16 <u>Graphics</u>.

a. Developers should use best commercial practices for graphics format and display.

b. Preferred vector graphics standard: CGM - WebCGM Type 4 Profile (which is moving towards an ISO Std.).

9.2.17 <u>Hardware User Interface (e.g., Point and Click, Voice, Selection Keys, A/N Keyboard, Touch Pad, etc.)</u>.

a. Point and click capability on target display should be assumed.

b. Developers should accommodate the limitations of the target display device.

c. Alphanumeric input capability should be provided, if not in hardware, then in software.

9.2.18 <u>Performance (Response Time by Context)</u>.

a. Developers should implement a less than 2-second response time goal.

b. If the response time is greater than 2 seconds, the system should provide visual feedback to the user (e.g., use a standard cursor for Processing Indication).

9.2.19 Printer Output.

a. Printed output is strongly discouraged.

b. Print capability should be used primarily for graphics.

c. All printer output should have version number and/or printed date/time stamp.

d. When customer needs printed output:

 1. Printer output should not have to conform to normal paper TM specifications

 2. Satisfactory Options:

  (a) "Pre-composed" files (such as Adobe PDF) can be attached.

  (b) "On-the-fly" composition for printing (of logical element) built into the viewing application.

  (c) Screen print. Preferred method: print data content of active window only.

9.2.20 User Annotations (e.g., comments, user notes, redlines, bookmarks).

a. There should be a persistent visual indication that an annotation exists.

b. The default initial presentation of annotations is to appear minimized.

c. If there are levels of annotations (e.g., public, private, etc.), they should be visually differentiated.

9.2.21 Feedback to Originator (e.g., TMDRS, Form-2028, AFTO 22).

a. A single user interaction should be available to select the function. (e.g., a button, double mouse click).

b. The preferred user interface is a form.

c. The system should provide an output compatible with the user environment.

d. There should be a "Form fill-in completed" function before returning to the IETM (e.g., "submit," "done," "okay," "close-out".)

e. The system should automatically generate an electronic locator (e.g., address, version) and to the greatest extent possible, relevant fields on the form should be automatically filled-in (e.g., user ID, system state, etc.).

9.2.22 <u>Administrative Information (e.g., effectivity, authorization, distribution, validation/verification)</u>. Administrative information should be displayable.

9.2.23 <u>Interface to External References and Systems</u>. A single user interaction should electronically link to external references (e.g., another IETM) or external systems (e.g., CAMS, IMDS, FEDLOG, GCSS, Supply Support/Parts Ordering, etc.).

9.2.24 <u>Rapid Action Changes and Critical Safety Interim Messages</u>.

a. A visual indication of the existence of a critical change should be displayed in context.

b. A single user interaction should be available to access the change.

c. The user should be provided with a visual indication for critical messages at the start of the IETM.

9.2.25 <u>Major Data Types (e.g., troubleshooting, procedural, parts, descriptive)</u>. Because of differences in user cultures and needs, this area cannot be addressed by providing guidance. Lessons learned may be a better way to address this category.

10.   NOTES

10.1   <u>Intended use</u>. This handbook is intended to be used as guidance for acquisition of electronic technical manuals, which includes both ETMs and IETMs and implementation of an environment for interoperable IETM products. This handbook applies to all Department of Defense (DoD) IETM acquisition and development activities. The handbook is also provided for the DoD policy officials and acquisition program managers who are responsible for policy and direction.

10.2   <u>Subject Term (Keyword) Listing</u>. The following terms are to be used to identify the MIL-HDBK-XXXX document during retrieval searches:

> Electronic addressing
> Electronic Technical Manual (ETM)
> eXtensible Markup Language
> eXtensible Style Language
> Interactive Electronic Technical Manual (IETM)
> interoperable
> Joint IETM Architecture
> object encapsulation
> presentation component
> Public Key Infrastructure (PKI)
> security
> stand-alone IETM
> virtual Uniform Resource Locator (vURL)

INDEX

	PARAGRAPH	**PAGE**

A

Acronyms	3.1	5
Addressing	8.3.4.1	50
Addressing in the occasionally connected mode	8.3.2	49
Addressing protocols	5.3.3	24
Addressing, Stand-alone Mode	8.4.3.1	53
Administrative Information	9.2.22	60
APPLICABLE DOCUMENTS	2.0	4
Application	1.2	1
Application Development Considerations	8.2.3	48
Architecture Applicability	5.2c	22
Architecture types S1 and S2	6.2b	28
Automated replication of Databases	8.3.5.2	51

B

Background	1.3	2
Background	7.1.1	35
Background	7.7.1	41
Basic Architecture	4.1.2	13
Browser -		
Classification	5.2	22
Overview	5.1	22
Salient Characteristics	5.3	23
Browser Capability	9.2.2	54
BROWSER COMPONENTS	5.0	22

C

C1 and C2 Architectures	6.2a	28
Cautions	9.2.7	56
Characteristics of JIA for User	4.2.1	13
Characteristics of JIA which should be preserved for future JIA	4.2	13
Classification	5.2	22
Client-based architecture properties	6.2.1	30
Commercially defined object model	5.3.2	24
Common Browser	4.3.1	18

	PARAGRAPH	PAGE

C (Cont)

Commonly used Addressing protocols	5.3.3	24
Commonly used Internet transport	5.3.3	24
Communication Security	4.4	20
Component Interface	4.3.2	19
Component Registry Description	7.7	41
Connectivity of IETMs	8.1.2	45
Context Filtering	9.2.10	57
Control Bars	9.2.4	54
Core object encapsulation	6.1	27
Cost Benefit Analysis	1.1	1
Critical Safety Interim Messages	9.2.24	60
Custom Server-side Applications/Extensions/DBs	8.3.5.1	50
Customized Server Applications and Extensions	8.2.1.2	46

D

Data Types	9.2.25	60
Data-base Driven IETMs in Occasionally Connected Mode	8.3.4	50
Database Server Interface	4.3.4	20
Database-driven IETM Applications	8.2.2	47
Database-driven IETM Apps in Stand-alone	8.4.2	52
Definitions of selected terms	3.2	7
DEFINITIONS	3.0	5
Deployment, General advisory for	6.2.3	33
Developer maintained JIA characteristics	4.2.2	16
Developing a solution for IETM Interoperability	4.1.3	13
Development Considerations - Stand-alone	8.4.3	53
Development Considerations	8.2.3	48
Development Considerations	8.3.5	50
Dialogs	9.2.13	58
Digital Signatures	5.3.9c	25
Display format	9.2.1	54
Distribution Code	3.2.1	7
DOD IETM Infrastructure Characteristics	4.2.3	16
Dual-Mode IETMs	4.5.2	21

	PARAGRAPH	**PAGE**

E

Element Addressing..	4.3.3	19
Element	3.2.2	8
Encryption	5.3.9b	25
End Item	3.2.3	8
End-User Interoperability.......................................	3.2.4	8
Entity	3.2.5	8
Environment	5.2b	22
Establishing & using vURLs......................................	7.3	39
Extensible Components...	5.3.5	24
eXtensible Markup Language	5.4.1	26
External Entity...	3.2.6	8
External Entity Addressing		
Catalog requirements..	7.2.4	38
Description	7.2.1	36
Features/Benefits..	7.2.2	37
Minimum Requirements.......................................	7.2.4	38
Salient Characteristics....................................	7.2	36
Specifications...	7.2.3	37
External references/systems, Interface to......................	9.2.23	60

F

Feedback to Originator..	9.2.21	59
File Pathname Locators for Legacy		
Applications	7.10	43
Frames	5.3.4	24

G

General advisory for deployment................................	6.2.3	33
GENERAL GUIDANCE..	4.0	10
General	2.1	4
General	7.1	35
Government Documents..	2.2	4
Graphics	9.2.16	58

H

Handbooks	2.2.1	4
Hardware User Interface	9.2.17	58
HTML Support..	5.3.8	25

	PARAGRAPH	**PAGE**

I

Icon Standardization	9.2.5	55
IETM ADDRESSING & REGISTRY SOFTWARE	7.0	35
IETM Architecture types C1 and C2	6.2a	28
IETM Component Registry Description	7.7	41
IETM Component	3.2.7	8
IETM object Metadata	7.4	41
IETM Object registry Features/Benefits	7.8	42
IETM Object Registry Specifications	7.9	43
IETM use in Stand-alone Environment	4.5	21
Implementing Advanced features	5.4	26
Information Access	9.2.12	57
Information Assurance Recommendations	4.4	20
Inline Link	3.2.8	8
Installation of Multiple DB Servers	8.2.3.2	48
Installation of Multiple Web Servers	8.2.3.2	48
Intended Use	10.1	60
Interface to External references/systems	9.2.23	60
Internet transport protocols	5.3.3	24
Intranet Server	4.3.4	20

J

Java Virtual Machine	5.3.10a	25
Java	5.3.10	25
Java	5.4.2	26
JIA -	8.1.1	44
Background	1.3	2
Basic Architecture	4.1.2	13
Characteristics for User	4.2.1	13
Characteristics to be kept	4.2	13
Developer maintained characteristics	4.2.2	16
DOD IETM Infrastructure	4.2.3	16
Object of JIA	1.3.2	3
Overall concept	4.1.1	10
Overview	4.1	10
Primary Goal	1.3.2	3
Recommendations for Implementation	4.3	18
Tri-Service Approach	1.3.1	3
Joint DOD/Industry User-Interaction		
Guidance	9.1	53
Just In Time Compiler	5.3.10b	25

	PARAGRAPH	**PAGE**

K

Keyword listing	10.2	60

L

Legacy Applications	7.10	43
Legacy IETM Systems	8.1.4	45
Library Functions	4.3.3	19
Life Cycle Support	7.1.5	36
Life Cycle Support	7.7.3	42
Link Behavior	9.2.3	54
Link	3.2.9	9
Linking and Addressing	8.3.4.1	50
Linking and Addressing, Stand-alone	8.4.3.1	53
Linking Elements	3.2.10	9
Locator	3.2.11	9
Logical Object	3.2.12	9

M

MAINTAINING A COMMON LOOK & FEEL	9.0	53
Major Data Types	9.2.25	60
Metadata	3.2.13	9
Metadata	7.5	41
Multimedia	5.3.12	26
Multiple data-base driven IETMs	8.3.4.2	50
Multiple Database-driven IETMs	8.4.3.2	53

N

Navigation	9.2.3	54
Networked Approach	8.2.1.1	46
Networked Client/Server Configuration F	8.2.1.3	47
Networked Client/Server IETM Apps	8.2	45
Non-Government Publications	2.3	5
NOTES	10.0	60
Notes	9.2.7	56
NSN	3.2.14	9

	PARAGRAPH	**PAGE**

O

Object encapsulation for various JIA types	6.2	27
OBJECT ENCAPSULATION GUIDANCE	6.0	26
Object Encapsulation	4.3.2	19
Object Model, Commercially defined	5.3.2	24
Object of JIA	1.3.2	3
Occasionally Connected applications	8.3	48
Occasionally connected mode - Addressing	8.3.2	49
Occasionally connected mode - Features	8.3.3	49
Occasionally-Connected user devices	4.5.1	21
Offline Browsing	5.3.7	24
Off-the-Shelf Web Servers	8.1.3	45
Operational Environments	7.1.3	35
Order of precedence	2.4	5
Other vURL attributes	7.2.6	37
Out-of-Line Link	3.2.15	9
Overall JIA Concept	4.1.1	10
Overview of JIA	4.1	10
Overview	5.1	22
Overview	8.1	44

P/Q

Performance	9.2.18	58
Personal Certificates	5.3.9a	25
Platform	5.2a	22
Primary Goal	1.3.2	3
Printer Output	9.2.19	59
Properties, Client-based architecture	6.2.1	30
Properties, Server-based architecture	6.2.2	31

R

Rapid Action Changes	9.2.24	60
Recommendations for Implementation	4.3	18
Regulatory requirements	5.5	26
Required operational capability	7.1.2	35
Required Operational Capability	7.7.2	42
Resource	3.2.16	9

	PARAGRAPH	**PAGE**

S

S1 and S2 Architectures	6.2b	28
Salient Characteristics	5.3	23
SCOPE	1.0	1
Scope	1.1	1
Screen resolution & color Guidelines	9.2.11	57
Search & Lookup	9.2.8	56
Search Engine	7.6	41
Security Environment	7.1.4	36
Security	5.3.9	25
Selectable Elements	9.2.6	56
Server Model	5.3.1	24
Server-based Architecture properties	6.2.2	31
Servers	8.2.3.1	48
Server-side applications	8.2.3.1	48
Service points of contact for vURL Requirements	7.11	44
Session Control	9.2.9	57
Sound	9.2.14	58
Specifications	2.2.1	4
Stand-alone Configuration Features	8.4.1.2	52
Stand-alone Environment, IETM Use in	4.5	21
Stand-alone IETM Applications	8.4	51
Stand-alone Mode - DB-Driven IETMs in	8.4.2	52
Standards	2.2.1	4
Subject term/Keyword listing	10.2	60
Supported Data Types	5.3.11	25

T

Target IETM Constituency	1.2	1
Technical Manual	3.2.17	9
Thin Client/Sever Model	5.3.1	24
Tri-Service Approach	1.3.1	3

U

Uniform Resource Identifier	3.2.18	9
URLs	7.10	43
User Annotations	9.2.20	59
User Interface	5.3.6	24

	PARAGRAPH	PAGE

U (Cont)

User Interface, hardware	9.2.17	58
User-Interaction Requirements for DOD IETMs	9.2	54

V

View Package	3.2.19	10
Virtual Uniform Resource Locator	3.2.20	10
Virtual Uniform Resource Locator	7.2.5	38
Voice Input/Output	9.2.15	58
vURL attributes	7.2.6	38
vURL registration, service POCS	7.11	44

W

Warnings, Cautions, Notes	9.2.7	56
Web Server Support - Stand-alone Mode	8.4.1	51
Web Server Support & Implementation	8.2.1	46
Web Server Support & Implementation	8.3.1	49
WEB SERVER/CLIENT/STAND-ALONE IMPLEMENTATION GUIDANCE	8.0	44
Web Servers & Stand-alone Configurations	8.4.1.1	51

X/Y/Z

XML	5.4.1	26

CONCLUDING MATERIAL

Custodian: Preparing Activity:

    Army – TM   Army - TM
    Navy – SH
    Air Force – 16   Project Number:

Review Activities: TMSS 0325

    Army – AL, AR, AT, AV, CR, CU, EA,
        MI, PT, PC3
    Navy – AS, CG, CH, EC, MC, TD
    Air Force – 8, 11, 13, 19, 22
    DLA - DH

This page intentionally left blank.

STANDARDIZATION DOCUMENT IMPROVEMENT PROPOSAL

I RECOMMEND A CHANGE	1.DOCUMENT NUMBER MIL-HDBK-511	2.DOCUMENT DATE *(YYMMDD)* 000515

3.DOCUMENT TITLE
DOD Handbook for Interoperability of Interactive Electronic Technical Manuals (IETMs)

4.NATURE OF CHANGE*(Identify paragraph number and include proposed rewrite, if possible. Attach extra sheets as needed.)*

5.REASON FOR RECOMMENDATION

6.SUBMITTER

a. NAME *(Last, First, Middle Initial)*	b. ORGANIZATION	
c. ADDRESS *(Include Zip Code)*	d. TELEPHONE (Include Area Code) (1)Commercial (2)AUTOVON(If applicable)	7.DATE SUBMITTED *(YYMMDD)*

8.PREPARING ACTIVITY

a. NAME USAMC Logistics Support Activity	b. TELEPHONE *(Include Area Code)* (1)Commercial (2)AUTOVON (256) 955-90852 645-0852
c. ADDRESS *(Include Zip Code)* ATTN: AMXLS-AP Redstone Arsenal, AL 35898-7466	IF YOU DO NOT RECEIVE A REPLY WITHIN 45 DAYS, CONTACT: Defense Standardization Program Office 8725 John J. Kingman Road, Suite 2533 Fort Belvoir, Virginia 22060-6221 Telephone (703) 767-6888 DSN 427-6888

www.ingramcontent.com/pod-product-compliance
Lightning Source LLC
Chambersburg PA
CBHW081409280526
45788CB00009B/3036